D0925638

NON SANZ DROICT.

William Shakespeare

THE WINTER'S TALE

Edited by Frank Kermode

The Signet Classic Shakespeare
GENERAL EDITOR: SYLVAN BARNET

A SIGNET CLASSIC from
NEW AMERICAN LIBRARY
TIMES MIRROR
New York and Toronto
The New English Library Limited, London

SIGNET TRADEMARK REG. U.S. PAT. OFF. AND FOREIGN COUNTRIES
REGISTERED TRADEMARK—MARCA REGISTRADA
HECHO EN CHICAGO, U.S.A.

SIGNET, SIGNET CLASSICS, SIGNETTE, MENTOR AND PLUME BOOKS
are published *in the United States* by
The New American Library, Inc.,
1301 Avenue of the Americas, New York, New York 10019,
in Canada by The New American Library of Canada Limited,
295 King Street East, Toronto 2, Ontario,
in the United Kingdom by The New English Library Limited,
Barnard's Inn, Holborn, London, E.C. 1, England

PRINTED IN THE UNITED STATES OF AMERICA

Contents

Shakespeare: Prefatory Remarks   *vii*

Introduction   *xxi*

The Winter's Tale   39

Textual Note   153

The Source of *The Winter's Tale*   155

   Selections from Robert Greene: *Pandosto*   157

Commentaries   178

   Simon Forman: *The Winter's Tale* at the
   Globe, 1611, the 15 of May   178

   Samuel Taylor Coleridge: [Comments on
   The Winter's Tale]   180

   E. M. W. Tillyard: From *Shakespeare's
   Last Plays*   184

   G. Wilson Knight: From *The Crown
   of Life*   193

   Wolfgang Clemen: From *The Development of Shakespeare's Imagery*   205

Suggested References   217

Shakespeare: Prefatory Remarks

Between the record of his baptism in Stratford on 26 April 1564 and the record of his burial in Stratford on 25 April 1616, some forty documents name Shakespeare, and many others name his parents, his children, and his grandchildren. More facts are known about William Shakespeare than about any other playwright of the period except Ben Jonson. The facts should, however, be distinguished from the legends. The latter, inevitably more engaging and better known, tell us that the Stratford boy killed a calf in high style, poached deer and rabbits, and was forced to flee to London, where he held horses outside a playhouse. These traditions are only traditions; they may be true, but no evidence supports them, and it is well to stick to the facts.

Mary Arden, the dramatist's mother, was the daughter of a substantial landowner; about 1557 she married John Shakespeare, who was a glovemaker and trader in various farm commodities. In 1557 John Shakespeare was a member of the Council (the governing body of Stratford), in 1558 a constable of the borough, in 1561 one of the two town chamberlains, in 1565 an alderman (entitling him to the appellation "Mr."), in 1568 high bailiff—the town's highest political office, equivalent to mayor. After 1577, for an unknown reason, he drops out of local politics. The birthday of William Shakespeare, the eldest son of this locally prominent man, is unrecorded; but the Stratford parish register records that the infant was baptized on 26 April 1564. (It is quite possible that he was born on 23 April, but this date has probably been assigned by tradition because it is the date on which, fifty-two years later, he died.) The attendance records of the Stratford grammar school of the period are not extant, but it is reasonable to assume that the son of a local official attended the school and received substantial training in Latin. The masters of the school from Shakespeare's seventh to fifteenth years held Oxford degrees; the Elizabethan curriculum excluded mathematics and the natural sciences but taught a good deal of Latin rhetoric, logic, and literature. On 27 November 1582 a marriage license was issued to Shakespeare and Anne Hathaway, eight years his senior. The couple had a child in May, 1583. Perhaps the marriage was necessary, but perhaps the couple had earlier engaged in a formal "troth-plight," which would render their children legitimate even if no further ceremony were performed. In 1585 Anne Hathaway bore Shakespeare twins.

That Shakespeare was born is excellent; that he married and had children is pleasant; but that we know nothing about his departure from Stratford to London, or about the beginning of his theatrical career, is lamentable and must be admitted. We would gladly sacrifice details about his children's baptism for details about his earliest days on the stage. Perhaps the poaching episode is true (but it is first reported almost a century after Shakespeare's death), or perhaps he first left Stratford to be a school-teacher, as another tradition holds; perhaps he was moved by

> Such wind as scatters young men through the world,
> To seek their fortunes further than at home
> Where small experience grows.

In 1592, thanks to the cantankerousness of Robert Greene, a rival playwright and a pamphleteer, we have our first reference, a snarling one, to Shakespeare as an actor and playwright. Greene warns those of his own educated friends who wrote for the theater against an actor who has presumed to turn playwright:

> There is an upstart crow, beautified with our feathers, that with his *tiger's heart wrapped in a player's hide*

supposes he is as well able to bombast out a blank verse as the best of you, and being an absolute Johannesfactotum is in his own conceit the only Shake-scene in a country.

The reference to the player, as well as the allusion to Aesop's crow (who strutted in borrowed plumage, as an actor struts in fine words not his own), makes it clear that by this date Shakespeare had both acted and written. That Shakespeare is meant is indicated not only by "Shakescene" but by the parody of a line from one of Shakespeare's plays, *3 Henry VI:* "O, tiger's heart wrapped in a woman's hide." If Shakespeare in 1592 was prominent enough to be attacked by an envious dramatist, he probably had served an apprenticeship in the theater for at least a few years.

In any case, by 1592 Shakespeare had acted and written, and there are a number of subsequent references to him as an actor: documents indicate that in 1598 he is a "principal comedian," in 1603 a "principal tragedian," in 1608 one of the "men players." The profession of actor was not for a gentleman, and it occasionally drew the scorn of university men who resented writing speeches for persons less educated than themselves, but it was respectable enough: players, if prosperous, were in effect members of the bourgeoisie, and there is nothing to suggest that Stratford considered William Shakespeare less than a solid citizen. When, in 1596, the Shakespeares were granted a coat of arms, the grant was made to Shakespeare's father, but probably William Shakespeare (who the next year bought the second-largest house in town) had arranged the matter on his own behalf. In subsequent transactions he is occasionally styled a gentleman.

Although in 1593 and 1594 Shakespeare published two narrative poems dedicated to the Earl of Southampton, *Venus and Adonis* and *The Rape of Lucrece,* and may well have written most or all of his sonnets in the middle nineties, Shakespeare's literary activity seems to have been almost entirely devoted to the theater. (It may be significant that the two narrative poems were written in years when the plague closed the theaters for several months.) In 1594 he was a charter member of a theatrical company called the Chamberlain's Men (which in 1603 changed its name to the King's Men); until he retired to Stratford (about 1611, apparently), he was with this remarkably stable company. From 1599 the company acted primarily at the Globe Theatre, in which Shakespeare held a one-tenth interest. Other Elizabethan dramatists are known to have acted, but no other is known also to have been entitled to a share in the profits of the playhouse.

Shakespeare's first eight published plays did not have his name on them, but this is not remarkable; the most popular play of the sixteenth century, Thomas Kyd's *The Spanish Tragedy,* went through many editions without naming Kyd, and Kyd's authorship is known only because a book on the profession of acting happens to quote (and attribute to Kyd) some lines on the interest of Roman emperors in the drama. What is remarkable is that after 1598 Shakespeare's name commonly appears on printed plays—some of which are not his. Another indication of his popularity comes from Francis Meres, author of *Palladis Tamia: Wit's Treasury* (1598): in this anthology of snippets accompanied by an essay on literature, many playwrights are mentioned, but Shakespeare's name occurs more often than any other, and Shakespeare is the only playwright whose plays are listed.

From his acting, playwriting, and share in a theater, Shakespeare seems to have made considerable money. He put it to work, making substantial investments in Stratford real estate. When he made his will (less than a month before he died), he sought to leave his property intact to his descendants. Of small bequests to relatives and to friends (including three actors, Richard Burbage, John Heminges, and Henry Condell), that to his wife of the second-best bed has provoked the most comment; perhaps it was the bed the couple had slept in, the best being reserved for visitors. In any case, had Shakespeare not excepted it, the bed would have gone (with the rest of his household possessions) to his daughter and her husband. On 25 April 1616 he was buried in the chancel of the church at Stratford. An unattractive monument to his memory, placed on a wall near the grave, says he died on 23 April. Over the grave itself are the lines, perhaps by Shakespeare, that (more than his literary fame) have kept his bones undisturbed in the crowded burial ground where old bones were often dislodged to make way for new:

> Good friend, for Jesus' sake forbear
> To dig the dust enclosèd here.
> Blessed be the man that spares these stones
> And cursed be he that moves my bones.

Thirty-seven plays, as well as some nondramatic poems, are held to constitute the Shakespeare canon. The dates of composition of most of the works are highly uncertain, but there is often evidence of a *terminus a quo* (starting point) and/or a *terminus ad quem* (terminal point) that provides a framework for intelligent guessing. For example, *Richard II* cannot be earlier than 1595, the publication date of some material to which it is indebted; *The Merchant of Venice* cannot be later than 1598, the year Francis Meres mentioned it. Sometimes arguments for a date hang on an alleged topical allusion, such as the lines about the unseasonable weather in *A Midsummer Night's Dream,* II.i.81–117, but such an allusion (if indeed it is an allusion) can be variously interpreted, and in any case there is always the possibility that a topical allusion was inserted during a revision, years after the composition of a play. Dates are often attributed on the basis of style, and although conjectures about style usually rest on other conjectures, sooner or later one must rely on one's literary sense. There is no real proof, for example, that *Othello* is not as early as *Romeo and Juliet,* but one feels *Othello* is later, and because the first record of its performance is 1604, one is glad enough to set its composition at that date and not push it back into Shakespeare's early years. The following chronology, then, is as much indebted to informed guesswork and sensitivity as it is to fact. The dates, necessarily imprecise, indicate something like a scholarly consensus.

PLAYS

1588–93	*The Comedy of Errors*
1588–94	*Love's Labor's Lost*
1590–91	*2 Henry VI*
1590–91	*3 Henry VI*
1591–92	*1 Henry VI*
1592–93	*Richard III*
1592–94	*Titus Andronicus*
1593–94	*The Taming of the Shrew*
1593–95	*The Two Gentlemen of Verona*
1594–96	*Romeo and Juliet*
1595	*Richard II*
1594–96	*A Midsummer Night's Dream*
1596–97	*King John*
1596–97	*The Merchant of Venice*
1597	*1 Henry IV*
1597–98	*2 Henry IV*
1598–1600	*Much Ado About Nothing*
1598–99	*Henry V*
1599–1600	*Julius Caesar*
1599–1600	*As You Like It*
1599–1600	*Twelfth Night*
1600–01	*Hamlet*
1597–1601	*The Merry Wives of Windsor*
1601–02	*Troilus and Cressida*
1602–04	*All's Well That Ends Well*
1603–04	*Othello*
1604–05	*Measure for Measure*
1605–06	*King Lear*
1605–06	*Macbeth*
1606–07	*Antony and Cleopatra*
1605–08	*Timon of Athens*
1607–09	*Coriolanus*
1608–09	*Pericles*
1609–10	*Cymbeline*
1610–11	*The Winter's Tale*
1611–12	*The Tempest*
1612–13	*Henry VIII*

POEMS

1592	*Venus and Adonis*
1593–94	*The Rape of Lucrece*
1593–1600	*Sonnets*
1600–01	*The Phoenix and Turtle*

Shakespeare's Theater

In Shakespeare's infancy, Elizabethan actors performed wherever they could—in great halls, at court, in the courtyards of inns. The innyards must have made rather unsatisfactory theaters: on some days they were unavailable because carters bringing goods to London used them as depots; when available, they had to be rented from the innkeeper; perhaps most important, London inns were subject to the Common Council of London, which was not well disposed toward theatricals. In 1574 the Common Council required that plays and playing places in London be licensed. It asserted that

> sundry great disorders and inconveniences have been found to ensue to this city by the inordinate haunting of great multitudes of people, specially youth, to plays, interludes, and shows, namely occasion of frays and quarrels, evil practices of incontinency in great inns having chambers and secret places adjoining to their open stages and galleries,

and ordered that innkeepers who wished licenses to hold performances put up a bond and make contributions to the poor.

The requirement that plays and innyard theaters be licensed, along with the other drawbacks of playing at inns, probably drove James Burbage (a carpenter-turned-actor) to rent in 1576 a plot of land northeast of the city walls and to build here—on property outside the jurisdiction of the city—England's first permanent construction designed for plays. He called it simply the Theatre. About all that is known of its construction is that it was of wood. It soon had imitators, the most famous being the Globe (1599), built across the Thames (again outside the city's jurisdiction), out of timbers of the Theatre, which had been dismantled when Burbage's lease ran out.

There are three important sources of information about the structure of Elizabethan playhouses—drawings, a contract, and stage directions in plays. Of drawings, only the so-called De Witt drawing (*c.* 1596) of the Swan—really a friend's copy of De Witt's drawing—is of much significance. It shows a building of three tiers, with a stage jutting from a wall into the yard, or center of the building. The tiers are roofed, and part of the stage is covered by a roof that projects from the rear and is supported at its front on two posts, but the groundlings, who paid a penny to stand in front of the stage, were exposed to the sky. (Performances in such a playhouse were held only in the daytime; artificial illumination was not used.) At the rear of the stage are two doors; above the stage is a gallery. The second major source of information, the contract for the Fortune, specifies that although the Globe is to be the model, the Fortune is to be square, eighty feet outside and fifty-five inside. The stage is to be forty-three feet broad and is to extend into the middle of the yard (i.e., it is twenty-seven and a half feet deep). For patrons willing to pay more than the general admission charged of the groundlings, there were to be three galleries provided with seats. From the third chief source, stage directions, one learns that entrance to the stage was by doors, presumably spaced widely apart at the rear ("Enter one citizen at one door, and another at the other"), and that in addition to the platform stage there was occasionally some sort of curtained booth or alcove allowing for "discovery" scenes, and some sort of playing space "aloft" or "above" to represent (for example) the top of a city's walls or a room above the street. Doubtless each theater had its own peculiarities, but perhaps we can talk about a "typical" Elizabethan theater if we realize that no theater need exactly have fit the description, just as no father is the typical father with 3.7 children. This hypothetical theater is wooden, round or polygonal (in *Henry V* Shakespeare calls it a "wooden *O*"), capable of holding some eight hundred spectators standing in the yard around the projecting elevated stage and some fifteen hundred additional spectators seated in the three roofed galleries. The stage, protected by a "shadow" or "heavens" or roof, is entered by two doors; behind the doors is the "tiring house" (attiring house, i.e., dressing room), and above the doors is some sort of gallery that may sometimes hold spectators but that can be used (for example) as the bedroom from which Romeo—according to a stage direction in one text—"goeth down." Some evidence suggests that a throne can be lowered onto the platform stage, perhaps from the "shadow"; certainly characters can descend from the stage through a trap or traps into the celler or "hell." Sometimes this space beneath the platform accommodates a sound-effects man or musician (in *Antony and Cleopatra* "music of the hautboys is under the stage") or an actor (in *Hamlet* the "Ghost cries under the stage"). Most characters simply walk on and off, but because there is no curtain in front of the platform, corpses will have to be carried off (Hamlet must lug Polonius' guts into the neighbor room) or will have to fall at the rear, where the curtain on the alcove or booth can be drawn to conceal them.

Such may have been the so-called "public theater." Another kind of theater, called the "private theater" because its much greater admission charge limited its audience to the wealthy or the prodigal, must be briefly mentioned. The private theater was basically a large room, entirely roofed, and therefore artificially illuminated, with a stage at one end. In 1576 one such theater was established in Blackfriars, a Dominican priory in London that had been suppressed in 1538 and confiscated by the Crown and thus was not under the city's jurisdiction. All the actors in the Blackfriars theater were boys about eight to thirteen years old (in the public theaters similar boys played female parts; a boy Lady Macbeth played to a man Macbeth). This private theater had a precarious existence and ceased operations in 1584. In 1596 James Burbage, who had already made theatrical history by building the Theatre, began to construct a second Blackfriars theater. He died in 1597, and for several years this second Blackfriars theater was used by a troupe of boys, but in 1608 two of Burbage's sons and five other actors (including Shakespeare) became joint operators of the theater, using it in the ensuing winters, when the open-air Globe was unsuitable. Perhaps such a smaller theater, roofed, artificially illuminated, and with a tradition of a courtly audience, exerted an influence on Shakespeare's late plays.

Performances in the private theaters may well have had intermissions, during which music was played, but in the public theaters the action was probably uninterrupted, flowing from scene to scene almost without a break. Actors would enter, speak, exit, and others would immediately enter and establish (if necessary) the new locale by a few properties and by words and gestures. Here are some samples of Shakespeare's scene painting:

> This is Illyria, lady.

> Well, this is the Forest of Arden.

> This castle hath a pleasant seat; the air
> Nimbly and sweetly recommends itself
> Unto our gentle senses.

On the other hand, it is a mistake to conceive of the Elizabethan stage as bare. Although Shakespeare's Chorus in *Henry V* calls the stage an "unworthy scaffold" and urges the spectators to "eke out our performance with your mind," there was considerable spectacle. The last act of *Macbeth,* for example, has five stage directions calling for "drum and colors," and another sort of appeal to the eye is indicated by the stage direction "Enter Macduff, with Macbeth's head." Some scenery and properties may have been substantial; doubtless a throne was used, and in one play of the period we encounter this direction: "Hector takes up a great piece of rock and casts at Ajax, who tears up a young tree by the roots and assails Hector." The matter is of some importance, and will be glanced at again in the next section.

The Texts of Shakespeare

Though eighteen of his plays were published during his lifetime, Shakespeare seems never to have supervised their publication. There is nothing unusual here; when a playwright sold a play to a theatrical company, he surrendered his ownership of it. Normally a company would not publish the play, because to publish it meant to allow competitors to acquire the piece. Some plays, however, did get published: apparently treacherous actors sometimes pieced together a play for a publisher, sometimes a company in need of money sold a play, and sometimes a company allowed a play to be published that no longer drew audiences. That Shakespeare did not concern himself with publication, then, is scarcely remarkable; of his contemporaries only Ben Jonson carefully supervised the publication of his own plays. In 1623, seven years after Shakespeare's death, John Heminges and Henry Condell (two senior members of Shakespeare's company, who had performed with him for about twenty years) collected his plays—published and unpublished—into a large volume, commonly called the First Folio. (A folio is a volume consisting of sheets that have been folded once, each sheet thus making two leaves, or four pages. The eighteen plays published during Shakespeare's lifetime had been issued one play per volume in small books called quartos. Each sheet in a quarto has been folded twice, making four leaves, or eight pages.) The First Folio contains thirty-six plays; a thirty-seventh, *Pericles,* though not in the Folio, is regarded as canonical. Heminges and Condell suggest in an address "To the great variety of readers" that the republished plays are presented in better form than in the quartos: "Before you were abused with diverse stolen and surreptitious copies, maimed and deformed by the frauds and stealths of injurious impostors that exposed them; even those, are now offered to your view cured and perfect of their limbs, and all the rest absolute in their numbers, as he [i.e., Shakespeare] conceived them."

Whoever was assigned to prepare the texts for publication in the First Folio seems to have taken his job seriously and yet not to have performed it with uniform care. The sources of the texts seem to have been, in general, good unpublished copies or the best published copies. The first play in the collection, *The Tempest,* is divided into acts and scenes, has unusually full stage directions and descriptions of spectacle, and concludes with a list of the characters, but the editor was not able (or willing) to present all of the succeeding texts so fully dressed. Later texts occasionally show signs of carelessness: in one scene of *Much Ado About Nothing* the names of actors, instead of characters, appear as speech prefixes, as they had in the quarto, which the Folio reprints; proofreading throughout the Folio is spotty and apparently was done without reference to the printer's copy; the pagination of *Hamlet* jumps from 156 to 257.

A modern editor of Shakespeare must first select his copy; no problem if the play exists only in the Folio, but a considerable problem if the relationship between a quarto and the Folio—or an early quarto and a later one—is unclear. When an editor has chosen what seems to him to be the most authoritative text or texts for his copy, he has not done with making decisions. First of all, he must reckon with Elizabethan spelling. If he is not producing a facsimile, he probably modernizes it, but ought he to preserve the old forms of words that apparently were pronounced quite unlike their modern forms—"lanthorn," "alablaster"? If he preserves these forms, is he really preserving Shakespeare's forms or perhaps those of a compositor in the printing house? What is one to do when one finds "lanthorn" and "lantern" in adjacent lines? (The editors of this series in general, but not invariably, assume that words should be spelled in their modern forms.) Elizabethan punctuation, too, presents problems. For example, in the First Folio, the only text for the play, Macbeth rejects his wife's idea that he can wash the blood from his hand:

> no: this my Hand will rather
> The multitudinous Seas incarnardine,
> Making the Greene one, Red.

Obviously an editor will remove the superfluous capitals, and he will probably alter the spelling to "incarnadine," but will he leave the comma before "red," letting Macbeth speak of the sea as "the green one," or will he (like most modern editors) remove the comma and thus have Macbeth say that his hand will make the ocean *uniformly* red?

An editor will sometimes have to change more than spelling or punctuation. Macbeth says to his wife:

> I dare do all that may become a man,
> Who dares no more, is none.

For two centuries editors have agreed that the second line is unsatisfactory, and have emended "no" to "do": "Who dares do more is none." But when in the same play Ross says that fearful persons

> floate vpon a wilde and violent Sea
> Each way, and moue,

need "move" be emended to "none," as it often is, on the hunch that the compositor misread the manuscript? The editors of the Signet Classics Shakespeare have restrained themselves from making abundant emendations. In their minds they hear Dr. Johnson on the dangers of emending: "I have adopted the Roman sentiment, that it is more honorable to save a citizen than to kill an enemy." Some departures (in addition to spelling, punctuation, and lineation) from the copy text have of course been made, but the original readings are listed in a note following the play so that the reader can evaluate them for himself.

The editors of the Signet Classic Shakespeare, following tradition, have added line numbers and in many cases act and scene divisions as well as indications of locale at the beginning of scenes. The Folio divided most of the plays into acts and some into scenes. Early-eighteenth-century editors increased the divisions. These divisions, which provide a convenient way of referring to passages in the plays, have been retained, but when not in the text chosen as the basis for the Signet Classic text, they are enclosed in square brackets [ ] to indicate that they are editorial additions. Similarly, although no play of Shakespeare's published during his lifetime was equipped with indications of locale at the heads of scene divisions, locales have here been added in square brackets for the convenience of the reader, who lacks the information afforded to spectators by costumes, properties, and gestures. The spectator can tell at a glance he is in the throne room, but without an editorial indication the reader may be puzzled for a while. It should be mentioned, incidentally, that there are a few authentic stage directions—perhaps Shakespeare's, perhaps a prompter's—that suggest locales: for example, "Enter Brutus in his orchard," and "They go up into the Senate house." It is hoped that the bracketed additions provide the reader with the sort of help provided in these two authentic directions, but it is equally hoped that the reader will remember that the stage was not loaded with scenery.

No editor during the course of his work can fail to recollect some words Heminges and Condell prefixed to the Folio:

> It had been a thing, we confess, worthy to have been wished, that the author himself had lived to have set forth and overseen his own writings. But since it hath been ordained otherwise, and he by death departed from that right, we pray you do not envy his friends the office of their care and pain to have collected and published them.

Nor can an editor, after he has done his best, forget Heminges and Condell's final words: "And so we leave you to other of his friends, whom if you need can be your guides. If you need them not, you can lead yourselves, and others. And such readers we wish him."

SYLVAN BARNET
Tufts University

Introduction

The Winter's Tale is a very late work of Shakespeare's, probably the last he wrote without a collaborator except for *The Tempest*; and it is universally supposed to be closely associated with *Cymbeline, The Tempest,* and *Pericles* (though this last play probably contains the work of another hand) in a grouping of comedies commonly called the "Romances." I have no intention of trying to overthrow this supposition; but it is worth recalling that the friends of Shakespeare who compiled the First Folio in 1623, far from thinking these plays should be read as a group, allowed them to be separated from each other to the limits of physical possibility. *The Tempest* is the first play in the Folio, heading the section of comedies; *The Winter's Tale* is the last of the comedies, and almost got left out altogether; *Cymbeline* comes last among the *tragedies*, and is the final play of the Folio; *Pericles* they did not include at all, and it was left to the editors of the Third Folio (1664) to insert it, together with six other plays that nobody now attributes to Shakespeare. But the long labors of the chronologists have brought together these scattered cousins; it is another "triumph of time," like *The Winter's Tale* itself. And this has prepared the way for much interesting comment on the group and the relations between its members. Still, the indifference or imperceptiveness of Heminges and Condell may at least serve as a caution. Much as the Romances resemble one another, they also exhibit striking differences; under the family resemblance, each has its private, personal life. The warning is so obvious as to be often ignored, and some

intemperate commentary has resulted. *The Winter's Tale*
has suffered with the others.

There is, for instance, the view—less common nowa-
days, but still to be met with—that these plays share a sort
of calm or detached simplicity, as if the author had sought
in Romance relief from the evils and disasters of the
tragedies. Now, the idea of romance, properly understood,
implies passion and catastrophe, storm and violence; and
Shakespeare's romances not only contain such elements,
but often enact them with much turbulence both in the
action and in the language. The verse frequently registers
not a gentle detachment but rather a remarkable activity
of mind. Thus the jealousy of Leontes may in the last
analysis be a less complex matter than that of Othello; but
it is less simply expressed. The language that embodies
it combines hysterical grossness with suggestions of a
mind once habituated to clarity but no longer quite able
to declare itself clearly because of emotional pressure:

> Ha' you not seen, Camillo—
> But that's past doubt, you have, or your eyeglass
> Is thicker than a cuckold's horn—or heard—
> For to a vision so apparent, rumor
> Cannot be mute—or thought—for cogitation
> Resides not in that man that does not think—
> My wife is slippery?

The evidence of Hermione's adultery is so overwhelming,
so disgusting, that an intelligent friend's failure to notice
it is an additional cause for anger. Leontes, accustomed to
putting his thoughts clearly, organizes what he has to
say in terms of sight, hearing, and reflection; but it would
be equally loathsome to hear Camillo fawningly agree or
disagree in order to dissuade him from the course of self-
torture to which he has committed himself. Thus contempt
and fear join with sexual disgust and an intolerable sense
of his own indignity to crowd and crush the speech, and
neither Elizabethan nor modern punctuation can cope
with its jolting syntax and distorted argument. Measure it
against the grave and by no means ill-written opening of
Greene's *Pandosto*: ". . . whoso seeks by friendly counsel

to raze out this hellish passion, it forthwith suspecteth that he giveth this advice to cover his own guiltiness. Yea, who-so is pained with this restless torment doubteth all, dis-trusteth himself, is always frozen with fear and fired with suspicion. . . ." Leontes in the play is ablaze with the passion of which Greene merely speaks. Or compare the same speech with Othello's after his fall into the same hell of sexual shock, reduced, when his agony is greatest, to broken exclamations: "O blood, blood, blood!" "Goats and monkeys!" Othello is not credited, as Leontes is, with an articulateness that matches his sense of self-destruction; he makes the great gestures appropriate to a noble under-standing of what it means for a hero's life to be broken— "Man but a rush against Othello's breast,/ And he retires" —but escapes the more intellectual torments of Leontes.[1]

Nor is this tumult of passionate meaning confined to moments of agony. It is a fair criticism of *Cymbeline* that there are places in it where the language is unnecessarily opaque, where—to quote Coleridge's definition of "men-tal bombast"—there are "thoughts and images too great for the subject." When Prospero tells Miranda, in *The Tempest,* of his brother's treachery, he can scarcely com-press his meaning in his excited utterance. In *The Winter's Tale* we feel the pressure of excited intelligence in many other speakers, as well as in Leontes, notably in Perdita and Florizel; their language breaks bounds in the quest for completeness of statement.

> What you do
> Still betters what is done. When you speak, sweet,

[1] I am not suggesting that *The Winter's Tale* has the stature of *Othello.* The tragedy has a different and perhaps a greater design; its focus is on the hero and the ideas by which he animates and gives value to his world; whereas the hero of *The Winter's Tale* is Time; or you might prefer to say that its heroine is Nature. The difference of emphasis may be suggested by one small indication. The word "honor" occurs with great frequency in *The Winter's Tale* to show that its characters are all necessarily concerned with this public acceptance of their own integrity; but the *idea* of honor is not at all stressed, as of course it is in *Othello,* and I myself had not noticed the frequent occurrence of the word until I gave the text slow editorial scrutiny. The main interests of the play lie in such a way that "honor" is a marginal, though necessary, consideration.

> I'd have you do it ever; when you sing,
> I'd have you buy and sell so; so give alms,
> Pray so; and for the ord'ring your affairs,
> To sing them too. When you do dance, I wish you
> A wave o' th' sea, that you might ever do
> Nothing but that, move still, still so,
> And own no other function. Each your doing,
> So singular in each particular,
> Crowns what you are doing in the present deeds,
> That all your acts are queens.

Florizel begins a catalogue of beauties, each more amorously and extravagantly expressed than its predecessor, and all related to action: "do," "done," "do," "doing," "function," "doing," "acts." He is drunk with the exquisite activity of Perdita. But he has a rhetorical scheme, and persists in it: each act is in itself perfect, yet each surpasses the other. This lover's hyperbole might ring out frigidly from the pages of Greene's novella, but here the whole scheme is transformed by the figure of the wave, a rich metaphor that the verse enacts rhythmically: "move still, still so"; until, at the end, the rhetorician's wit glows with imaginative solemnity, for "queens" not only concludes the prescribed scheme but moves us out beyond it, into the sphere where Perdita, singing and dancing, queen of the feast and dressed as a goddess of spring's renewal, assumes the power to end by her action the hard grip of winter on the lives of her parents.

Such verse makes ridiculous the notion of an author grown vaguely benign with old age; and it is to be found in all the Romances. There are other common features. In every play there is a discovery of lost royalty, princesses who are represented as of almost divine virtue and beauty; characters near death are restored to life; the breach in some prince's life is mended, years after the disaster which caused it, by the agency of young, beautiful, and innocent people; there are scenes of a pastoral character. All this is of the nature of Romance, and the plays could well be called romantic tragicomedies. Edwin Greenlaw long ago pointed out that they derive ultimately from the Greek novel, especially perhaps from *Daphnis and Chloe*. This is the world of lost princesses, great storms that sunder families, lifetimes spent in wandering or suffering, babies put to sea in little boats (an experience that belonged to Perdita, in the source story, though Shakespeare saved it for Miranda) and later recognized by a mole or a jewel. Greene's *Pandosto*, on which Shakespeare based his *Winter's Tale*, is a typical Elizabethan novel in the same tradition. And these plays are dramatic versions of such stories.

Shakespeare had used elements of romance plot as early as *The Comedy of Errors*; in returning to it he handles it with a new simplicity, especially in *The Winter's Tale*. He has no more compunction than a novelist might have in allowing sixteen years to pass in the middle of the story. But this is not because he couldn't help it, because his technique had gone soft. Stories of this kind are in their nature somewhat primitive, and if profundities are to be found in them it will be by the writer who respects their nature. It required much lucidity and experience to design *The Winter's Tale* so simply. "Shakespeare," Northrop Frye has said, "arrived in his last period at the bedrock of drama, the romantic spectacle out of which all the more specialized forms of drama, such as tragedy and social comedy, have come, and to which they recurrently return." Of course there are very bad romance plays, some of them in the repertory of Shakespeare's company at this period. Merely using an archaic narrative ensures no big bonus of significance. That is the reward of genius, and of a lifetime of intelligent practice. I daresay Shakespeare might have been surprised to read in Frye that his Hermione is a "Proserpine figure," but not to hear that he had told his story in such a way that we see human life renewing itself, as spring follows winter. He even suggests the relevance of the well-known Proserpine myth in Perdita's flower speech. He is writing, with very conscious art, about the destruction and renewal of life, and finds in these romance stories the pattern he needs; it is his craft to elicit and enlarge their relevance.

It is perfectly consistent to add that Shakespeare was probably writing to meet a specific public demand (as the revival of an old and bad romance, *Mucedorus*, suggests). With similar opportunism, he probably used in the fourth act dances that his company had performed under grander circumstances at court. He may also have had in mind the Blackfriars, his company's new indoor theater, where from about 1609 they enjoyed the advantages of a smaller house with better music, good artificial lighting, scenes and machines, and an audience willing to pay six times the price of the cheapest place at the Globe. This was the time of the spectacular masques at the court of James I; Shakespeare's company were the King's Men; never had relations between court and stage been closer than now. They continued to play in the great outdoor theater; but possibly the Blackfriars, where some of the courtly spectacle could be reproduced, had something to do with the vogue for extravagant romance stories.

Yet this is not the most important clue to the nature of *The Winter's Tale*. For that we should turn to the greatest works in prose and verse of the period, Sidney's *Arcadia* and Spenser's *Faerie Queene*. It is no reflection on Greene to say that his novel cannot live with such romances as these; for they are in intention and performance the profoundest and most serious art of the period (Spenser's book, to risk a comparison for the modern reader, is as complex in plan as *Ulysses*). They nevertheless use romantic themes. They are concerned less with psychological realism than with supernaturally sanctioned reality under human appearances. Shakespeare knew them both, and used them, especially Spenser. Marina is his Florimel, Perdita his Pastorella; in *The Winter's Tale* he transforms Fawnia, Greene's royal changeling, and does so to make her like Spenser's noble shepherdess. And insofar as *The Winter's Tale* is philosophical it is Spenserian too; like Spenser, Shakespeare is preoccupied by Time as destroyer and renewer, that which ruins the work of men but is the father of truth. Just as the sea appears to be aimlessly destructive, tearing apart father and child, husband and wife, but is in the end seen to be "merciful" because it finally brings them together and restores their happiness, so Time only seems to change things because it must renew their truth.

> All things steadfastness do hate
> And changed be: yet being rightly weighed
> They are not changed from their first estate,
> But by their change their being do dilate,
> And turning to themselves at length again,
> Do work their own perfection so by fate.

Whatever else may be added on the point, this is the "philosophy" of *The Winter's Tale* as well as of the Mutability Cantos of Spenser. And Greene, to give him his due, called the novel on which Shakespeare based his play *Pandosto: or, The Triumph of Time*.

One more point before we turn from the romances in general to the specific qualities of *The Winter's Tale*: stories of this kind create for the dramatist peculiar technical problems. Characteristically, they require that there be treated the initial disaster by which the plot gains movement; the intermediate period where people suffer under the consequent wrongs and sorrows; and finally the restoration of happiness, the *recognition*, where all, by the work of time, "turns to itself at length again." Dramatically, the focus of such stories will tend to be the recognition; in *Pericles*, a very straggling play, this climax was what overwhelmingly interested Shakespeare, and he made it a kind of prototype of all the others. In *Cymbeline* he attempted a multiple recognition scene so extraordinary as to be without theatrical parallel. In *The Tempest* he concentrates the whole action at the moment of climax, merely recalling the initial treachery of Antonio. In *The Winter's Tale* he approaches the problem quite differently by dividing the story into three parts: first the Sicilian disaster, the destruction of happiness by Leontes' diseased passion; then the "green world" in which Perdita demonstrates renewed beauty and nobility (these two parts being equally balanced as to length); and finally an act of recognition. Though the great scene in *Pericles* is the ancestor of them all, the recognition scenes of these plays are all very different, and this of course contributes to their individuality, the sense we have that each grows its own imaginative and philosophical atmosphere. And nowhere is this atmosphere more distinctive, nowhere is the recognition more daringly conceived, than in *The Winter's Tale*.

Some indication of the dramatist's intention, both in this and in other aspects of the play, may be derived from a consideration of the changes he made in his source. A large part of Greene's *Pandosto* is printed at the end of this volume, and the reader may see for himself the extent of both debt and deviation; a few editorial words on the matter are prefixed to the extracts. But on the crucial matter of the great final act something must be said here. The statue scene is without parallel in *Pandosto;* at some stage Shakespeare made the momentous decision to keep Hermione alive, and invented the *motif* of the statue. It is possible that he did so in the course of writing; as Coleridge early pointed out, it would have been simple enough to provide for her survival by some ambiguity in the oracle, but Shakespeare does not do so, and it is a remarkable instance, the only one in Shakespeare or perhaps in the whole drama of the period, of the playwright's concealing so material a circumstance from the audience. Simon Forman, reporting on a performance of 1611 when the play was still fairly new, did not include in his account of the plot any allusion to the statue scene, so the play may have been without it in its first form. Having preserved Hermione alive, Shakespeare had of course greatly increased his technical problem at the end of the play. Had he followed Greene, the climactic moment would have been the discovery of Perdita's identity, and the scene would have had to be very like that of the reunion of Pericles and Marina. He could hardly have followed this with another scene of rapt verse and music for the reunion of Leontes and his wife; so he boldly throws away the Perdita recognition in a scene of gentlemanly chatter, and saves the great effects for the reunion of father, mother, and daughter at the end. Thus he avoids the anticlimactic conclusion of *Pericles*, where the reunion with Thaisa cannot make much effect after the great scene that precedes it. So Shakespeare solved his technical problem; the question remains, why did he need to create it by forsaking Greene and keeping Hermione alive? Why should the climax of the play be not the restoration of Perdita to her inheritance but the restoration of the Queen to life? No one can answer that without looking at the play as a whole.

The whole work is as unorthodox structurally as the final scene. The first part, up to the end of III.ii, is dominated by the insane and tyrannous passion of Leontes. The Sicilian court has been a world of courtesy and innocence; these are virtues of Hermione and also of Polixenes, whose opening speech, with its pastoral figures, merely establishes an intelligent harmony that will be broken by the power of the diseased king. Polixenes remembers the innocence of his childhood friendship with Leontes, and says it resembled that of man before the Fall, when passion overthrew reason; and with the onset of the King's jealousy this overthrow is re-enacted. It is clumsy to treat this as pure allegory, though that is a modern fashion; Shakespeare knew very well that there was implied in this narrative an analogy with the Fall, and he lived in an age when Biblical typology and allegory were as familiar as they now seem outlandish. But this should lead us to the conclusion, not that he was writing allegory, but that he was recognizing the *typical* quality of this, as of any other story. A powerful mind is disturbed by a passion it is unwilling to control; suddenly the clear world of honor and courtesy darkens; friends can be Judases, good counselors traitors; what seems to be virtuous is in truth vicious; the gods themselves are liars. Here as elsewhere Shakespeare associates this profound perturbation, this infection of a world with the disease of one mind, with a specifically sexual misery. For Leontes—the word tolls out through these scenes—is diseased, and the air around him is infected, as if by a plague-bearing planet. His very language is hectic. That there is another and purer air we learn from the brief, beautifully placed III.i, when Cleomenes and Dion speak of the delicate climate and sweet air of Apollo's temple. And when, sixteen years later, we breathe the air of Perdita's pastoral Bohemia we recognize once more a purity associated with pure sexuality; as when Perdita wishes her lover "quick, and in mine arms." The country, its healing herbs and prophylactic flowers, is the antithesis of the plague-stricken city. And later, when Perdita arrives in Sicily, Leontes remembers the days of the great infection and prays accordingly:

> The blessèd gods
> Purge all infection from our air whilst you
> Do climate here!

In the dark opening phase, the part of Hermione is that of the victim, Leontes that of the tyrant. Tyranny begins, as Milton says, "when upstart passions catch the government." But he considers and rejects the idea that he is behaving tyrannously; she, at her trial (which must recall the trial of Katherine in *Henry VIII*), argues that he is. His rejection of the oracle is a tyrannous act (Greene's *Pandosto* accepts it), and he at once suffers the traditional fate of the tyrant, the sudden exemplary punishment of heaven. His son dies, his queen dies; henceforth his life must be only repentance and obloquy. Or so it seems. At the end of III.ii, halfway through the play, we have reached what is practically a full tragic close, and if Leontes were to stab himself at that point there would be little sense of dramatic illogic. He has thrown away the pearl richer than all his tribe. Only the hint of the oracle ("*if* that which is lost be not found") and the fact that in romance castaway children always turn up, exist to make a faint suggestion of a happy issue.

The next scene, III.iii, is crucial, and again extraordinary; Antigonus, having had a vision of the *dead* Hermione, is sacrificed in order to move the play into a fantastic realm; the clown and his father show us how different is the world we have entered by the unconcerned calm of their talk on the sinking of the ship and the bear's consumption of Antigonus. Then the old man speaks the famous line: "Now bless thyself; thou met'st with things dying, I with things new born." We pass from the world in which happiness and prosperity are destroyed by the storm of passion, to the world where nature—great creating Nature, as Shakespeare calls the presiding figure of the Mutability Cantos—re-establishes love and human continuance and proves that time and change are her servants, agents not only of change but of perpetuity, redeemers as well as destroyers.

The central action of Act IV is not complicated, but it is a very long act, and must have been the longer for the various diversions, the "nest of antics" ridiculed by Jonson, the catches and songs. The mood is of innocence (even Autolycus contributes to this, partly by establishing rustic virtues as opposed to those of the court—an old pastoral theme, and one paralleled by the debates between Corin and Touchstone in *As You Like It*), and Shakespeare wanted this part of the play to have mass enough to balance the Sicilian opening. Essentially, this act establishes a world in which Perdita's inborn nobility can display itself.

Although Shakespeare accepts some of the assumptions of the pastoral genre, it was clearly his effort to avoid urban condescension and sentimentality in this scene. These shepherds and shepherdesses are not the graceful figures of Spenser and Sidney; the young clown has his meanness, the old one his strong sense of self-preservation; Polixenes is charmed by the feast and by Perdita's beauty, but when the holiday is over his exposure of the girl and his judgment of his son are extremely tough. Against this infused realism, the insistence upon Perdita's superiority, her innate nobility and godlike beauty, becomes more remarkable. It is, considered merely as a narrative device, part of the tradition, but it occupied Shakespeare at a very deep level. There are signs of his interest in it at an earlier stage in his career, but in the Romances he turned upon it the same deepening attention as we observe him giving such conventions as the twin plot—that which was first only a dramaturgical device becomes an issue for mature meditation. Marina in the brothel, Cymbeline's sons in the Welsh cave have the virtue of high birth, and their hereditary cultivation will show itself even in unfavorable circumstances. In *The Tempest* Caliban is the base natural stock, Miranda (educated with him) has, as part of her inheritance, that "better nature" which places her on the side of mankind toward the gods, as he is on the side toward the beasts.[2] Perdita, like all the Romance heroines mistaken for a goddess, is, very remarkably, made the occasion for Shakespeare's fullest exposition of the idea. It is characteristic of Shakespeare's economy that her flower piece, which could have been a moment of pastoral prettiness, modulates into this quasi-philosophical debate with Polixenes:

Perdita. Sir, the year growing ancient,
 Not yet on summer's death nor on the birth
 Of trembling winter, the fairest flow'rs o' th' season
 Are our carnations and streaked gillyvors,
 Which some call Nature's bastards; of that kind
 Our rustic garden's barren; and I care not
 To get slips of them.

Polixenes.   Wherefore, gentle maiden,
 Do you neglect them?

Perdita.   For I have heard it said,
 There is an art, which in their piedness shares
 With great creating Nature.

Polixenes.   Say there be;
 Yet Nature is made better by no mean,
 But Nature makes that mean; so over that art
 Which you say adds to Nature, is an art
 That Nature makes. You see, sweet maid, we marry
 A gentler scion to the wildest stock,
 And make conceive a bark of baser kind

---

[2] This point is discussed and documented in my Arden edition of *The Tempest* (6th ed. rev.). Cambridge, Mass.: Harvard University Press; London: Methuen & Co., Ltd., 1958.

By bud of nobler race. This is an art
Which does mend Nature, change it rather; but
The art itself is Nature.

Perdita.   So it is.

Polixenes. Then make your garden rich in gillyvors,
And do not call them bastards.

Perdita.   I'll not put
The dibble in earth, to set one slip of them;
No more than were I painted, I would wish
This youth should say 'twere well, and only therefore
Desire to breed by me.

In this disagreement Polixenes only *seems* to win,
though he has the general weight of contemporary thought
on his side; the art of the gardener in improving wild
natural stocks was treated as a figure of the distinctive
human power to improve and civilize the environment,
and it was customary to add that in so doing Art was nevertheless the agent of Nature. Perdita does not know she is
herself noble, and is only playing at being a queen,
though the audience has already noted strong suggestions
of her royalty, indeed of her semidivinity; and there is a
purely dramatic irony in the discussion, since Polixenes
is to oppose the union of his noble son with a supposedly
base-born girl, thus contradicting his own philosophy;
whereas she, base-born and hoping to marry a prince,
resists his horticultural analogy. Her case is precisely
that of Marvell in his poem "The Mower against Gardens,"
in which the gardener is called not an improver of nature
but a pander; but Perdita, unable to answer the argument
from gardening, produces one from cosmetics ("the gillyvors are like painted women") and so tacitly rejects the
implied resemblance between herself and "barks of baser
kind." Leaving aside the purely dramatic ironies, this
debate is one on which the arguments on both sides were
well known, and Shakespeare's purpose is not to identify
himself with one or other side so much as to tell the
audience that the great topic of the relations between
art and nature are relevant to his purposes; to establish

in every word as well as every action the "better nature" of Perdita, and to prepare the way for a climactic scene in which, when the statue proves to be powerful and beautiful beyond the scope of art, we shall see finally the incomparable work of "great creating Nature." Whenever he includes discussion of this kind—as he does, for example, in *The Merchant of Venice,* in *Troilus and Cressida,* in *Measure for Measure*—we may expect it to have its repercussions on the action. In this play we find them in the last act.

The pattern of this act is determined, as we have seen, by the need for a double recognition, but nothing at the level of plot required the dramatist to bring Hermione back into the play as a statue. Admittedly the scene lends itself to that tone of exalted joy which distinguishes these late plays of reunion, and is magnificently theatrical; having once committed himself to the situation the old master makes the most of the chance, holds us to the long moment of Hermione's immobility, and when it is over, concludes the play with what must appear, unless the producer has the necessary sensitivity and tact, unseemly haste. But as usual he makes theatrical effect compatible with thematic interest. Paulina soaks her guests in art by taking them on an extended tour round the gallery before she lets them see the statue. They praise it for its naturalness, its "life," while she protests that the color is still wet and calls it a "poor image." "What was he that did make it?" asks Leontes in unconscious tribute to the god of nature. The work is so "alive," he says, "that we are mocked with art." Slowly the statue moves out of the possibilities of art: "what fine chisel / Could ever yet cut breath?" Then it moves indeed, and the hypothesis that this is art can only be defended by calling that art magic. Finally it speaks, and blesses Perdita, and this no work of art, but only those of great creating nature, can do.

In its identification of the thematic and the theatrical, this is a true work of Shakespeare's. It is, of course, more complex than my account suggests. The survival of Hermione authenticates Perdita's beauty; time, which has seemed the destroyer, is a redeemer. At one masterly moment Perdita herself stands like a statue beside the supposed statue of her mother, to remind us that created things work their own perfection and continuance in time, as well as suffer under it. And in the end the play seems to say (I borrow the language of Yeats) that "whatever is begotten, born and dies" is nobler than "monuments of unageing intellect"—and also, when truly considered, more truly lasting.

Such a formula may justly attract the complaint that it is partial and moralizing. The play is a great one, with a natural energy that supports all it says about natural power; its scheme is deep-laid and its language fertile in suggestion. It will not be trapped by the historian, though he can speak of the vogue of tragicomic romance and compare Perdita with Pastorella. It will not, either, be caught in the net of allegory. To say that Hermione suffers, dies, and is restored to life, is not to suggest a parallel that the author missed, but equally not to hit his true intention. All truths, he might argue, are related to the Truth; all good stories will have—to use the term of Erich Auerbach—a "figural" quality. *The Winter's Tale,* like many other stories, deals with sin and forgiveness, and with the triumph of time—also a Christian theme. But we value it not for some hidden truth, but for its power to realize experience, to show something of life that could only be shown by the intense activity of intellect and imagination in the medium of a theatrical form. It is not a great allegory or a great argument, but a great play.

FRANK KERMODE
University of Manchester

The Winter's Tale

The Names of the Actors

Leontes, King of Sicilia
Mamillius, young Prince of Sicilia
Camillo
Antigonus
Cleomenes } four Lords of Sicilia
Dion
Hermione, Queen to Leontes
Perdita, daughter to Leontes and Hermione
Paulina, wife to Antigonus
Emilia, a Lady [attending on Hermione]
Polixenes, King of Bohemia
Florizel, Prince of Bohemia
Old Shepherd, reputed father of Perdita
Clown, his son
Autolycus, a rogue
Archidamus, a Lord of Bohemia
[A Mariner]
[A Jailer]
[Mopsa
 Dorcas } shepherdesses]
Other Lords and Gentlemen, [Ladies, Officers of the
   Court,] and Servants
Shepherds and Shepherdesses
[Time, as Chorus]
              [*Scene:* Sicilia and Bohemia]

The Winter's Tale

ACT I

Scene I. [*Sicilia, the Court of Leontes.*]

Enter Camillo and Archidamus.

Archidamus. If you shall chance, Camillo, to visit
Bohemia, on the like occasion whereon my services
are now on foot, you shall see, as I have said, great
difference betwixt our Bohemia and your Sicilia.

Camillo. I think this coming summer the King of   5
Sicilia means to pay Bohemia the visitation which
he justly owes him.

Archidamus. Wherein our entertainment shall shame
us we will be justified in our loves;° ¹ for indeed——

Camillo. Beseech you——   10

Archidamus. Verily I speak it in the freedom of my
knowledge: we cannot with such magnificence—
in so rare—I know not what to say. . . . We will
give you sleepy drinks, that your senses, unintel-
ligent° of our insufficience, may, though they can-   15
not praise us, as little accuse us.

¹ The degree sign (°) indicates a footnote, which is keyed to the text by
the line number. Text references are printed in *italic* type; the annota-
tion follows in roman type. I.i.8–9 *Wherein . . . loves* our entertainment
may fall short of yours, but we shall make up for it by the strength of
our affection   14–15 *unintelligent* unaware

Camillo. You pay a great deal too dear for what's given freely.

Archidamus. Believe me, I speak as my understanding
20 instructs me, and as mine honesty puts it to utterance.

Camillo. Sicilia cannot show himself overkind to Bohemia. They were trained together in their child-
hoods; and there rooted betwixt them then such
25 an affection, which cannot choose but branch° now.
Since their more mature dignities and royal necessities made separation of their society,° their en-
counters, though not personal, have been royally
attorneyed° with interchange of gifts, letters, lov-
30 ing embassies, that they have seemed to be together,
though absent: shook hands, as over a vast;° and
embraced as it were from the ends of opposed winds.
The heavens continue their loves!

Archidamus. I think there is not in the world either
35 malice or matter to alter it. You have an unspeakable
comfort of your young Prince Mamillius; it is a gentleman of the greatest promise that ever came into
my note.

Camillo. I very well agree with you in the hopes of
40 him. It is a gallant child; one that, indeed, physics
the subject,° makes old hearts fresh; they that went
on crutches ere he was born desire yet their life to
see him a man.

Archidamus. Would they else be content to die?

45 *Camillo.* Yes, if there were no other excuse why they
should desire to live.

Archidamus. If the King had no son, they would
desire to live on crutches till he had one.

Exeunt.

25 *branch* i.e., flourish 27 *society* companionship 29 *attorneyed* supplied
by substitutes 31 *vast* desolate space 40–41 *physics the subject* is good
medicine for the people

Scene II. [*The Court of Leontes.*]

Enter Leontes, Hermione, Mamillius, Polixenes,
Camillo, [and Attendants].

Polixenes. Nine changes of the wat'ry star° hath been
　　The shepherd's note since we have left our throne
　　Without a burden: time as long again
　　Would be filled up, my brother, with our thanks,
　　And yet we should for perpetuity   5
　　Go hence in debt. And therefore, like a cipher,
　　Yet standing in rich place, I multiply
　　With one "We thank you," many thousands moe°
　　That go before it.°

Leontes.　　　　　　　　Stay your thanks awhile,
　　And pay them when you part.   10

Polixenes.　　　　　　　　　　Sir, that's tomorrow.
　　I am questioned by my fears of what may chance
　　Or breed upon our absence, that may blow
　　No sneaping winds at home, to make us say,
　　"This is put forth too truly."° Besides, I have stayed
　　To tire your royalty.

Leontes.　　　　　　　We are tougher, brother,   15
　　Than you can put us to 't.°

I.ii.¹ *wat'ry star* i.e., the moon　⁸ *moe* more　³⁻⁹ *time as long . . . before it* it would take us the same length of time to thank you, and even
then we should leave here forever your debtors. So I offer you one more
thank-you, which, though it is in itself nothing, works like a zero on the
end of a number and multiplies all the thanks I've given you before
(instead of merely adding to them)　¹¹⁻¹⁴ *I am questioned . . . too
truly* i.e., I'm worried about what may happen at home, perhaps as a
result of my absence—worried in case blighting influences may not be
at work which we shall regret, saying "We went away only too well"
¹⁶ *put us to 't* drive us to extremities

Polixenes.   No longer stay.

Leontes. One sev'night longer.

Polixenes.   Very sooth, tomorrow.

Leontes. We'll part the time between 's then; and in
     that
     I'll no gainsaying.°

Polixenes.   Press me not, beseech you, so.
     There is no tongue that moves, none, none i' th'
20   world
     So soon as yours could win me; so it should now,
     Were there necessity in your request, although
     'Twere needful I denied it. My affairs
     Do even drag me homeward; which to hinder
25   Were, in your love, a whip to me;° my stay,
     To you a charge and trouble: to save both,
     Farewell, our brother.

Leontes.   Tongue-tied, our Queen? Speak you.

Hermione. I had thought, sir, to have held my peace
     until
     You had drawn oaths from him not to stay. You,
     sir,
30   Charge him too coldly. Tell him you are sure
     All in Bohemia's well; this satisfaction,
     The bygone day proclaimed. Say this to him,
     He's beat from his best ward.°

Leontes.   Well said, Hermione.

Hermione. To tell he longs to see his son were strong;
35   But let him say so then, and let him go;
     But let him swear so, and he shall not stay,
     We'll thwack him hence with distaffs.
     Yet of your royal presence, I'll adventure
     The borrow of a week. When at Bohemia
40   You take my lord, I'll give him my commission

---

¹⁹ *I'll no gainsaying* I'll not accept a refusal   ²⁵ *Were . . . to me* i.e.,
though doing it out of love, you would be tormenting me by making
me stay in these circumstances   ³³ *ward* defensive posture in fencing

  To let him there a month behind the gest°
  Prefixed for 's parting, yet, good deed,° Leontes,
  I love thee not a jar° o' th' clock behind
  What lady she° her lord. You'll stay?

Polixenes.   No, madam.

Hermione. Nay, but you will?

Polixenes.   I may not, verily.   45

Hermione. Verily?
  You put me off with limber° vows; but I,
  Though you would seek t' unsphere the stars with
      oaths,
  Should yet say, "Sir, no going." Verily,
  You shall not go; a lady's "Verily" is   50
  As potent as a lord's. Will you go yet?
  Force me to keep you as prisoner,
  Not like a guest; so you shall pay your fees°
  When you depart, and save your thanks. How say
      you?
  My prisoner or my guest? By your dread "Verily,"   55
  One of them you shall be.

Polixenes.   Your guest, then, madam:
  To be your prisoner should import offending;°
  Which is for me less easy to commit,
  Than you to punish.

Hermione.   Not your jailer, then,
  But your kind hostess. Come, I'll question you   60
  Of my lord's tricks, and yours, when you were boys:
  You were pretty lordings then?

Polixenes.   We were, fair Queen,
  Two lads that thought there was no more behind°
  But such a day tomorrow as today,
  And to be boy eternal.

Hermione.   Was not my lord   65
  The verier wag o' th' two?

---

⁴¹ *gest* stage of royal progress; time allocated to one place on the route
⁴² *good deed* indeed, in very deed   ⁴³ *jar* tick   ⁴⁴ *lady she* gentlewoman
⁴⁷ *limber* limp   ⁵³ *fees* (which were always due from prisoner to jailer)
⁵⁷ *import offending* mean that I had committed some crime   ⁶³ *behind*
to come

Polixenes. We were as twinned lambs, that did frisk
    i' th' sun,
    And bleat the one at th' other; what we changed°
    Was innocence for innocence; we knew not
70   The doctrine of ill-doing, nor dreamed
    That any did; had we pursued that life,
    And our weak spirits ne'er been higher reared
    With stronger blood, we should have answered
      heaven
    Boldly, "not guilty"; the imposition cleared,
    Hereditary ours.°

75 *Hermione.*   By this we gather
    You have tripped since.

    Polixenes.   O my most sacred lady,
    Temptations have since then been born to 's, for
    In those unfledged days was my wife a girl;
    Your precious self had then not crossed the eyes
    Of my young playfellow.

80 *Hermione.*   Grace to boot!°
    Of this make no conclusion,° lest you say
    Your queen and I are devils. Yet go on,
    Th' offenses we have made you do we'll answer,
    If you first sinned with us, and that with us
    You did continue fault, and that you slipped not
    With any but with us.

85 *Leontes.*   Is he won yet?

    Hermione. He'll stay, my lord.

    Leontes.   At my request he would not.
    Hermione, my dearest, thou never spok'st
    To better purpose.

    Hermione.   Never?

---

⁶⁸ *changed* exchanged   ⁷²⁻⁷⁵ *our weak spirits . . . Hereditary ours* i.e.,
had the weakness of our animal spirits not been fortified by the passionate blood of maturity, our wills would never have been corrupted,
and we should have been able to claim exemption from the taint of
original sin   ⁸⁰ *Grace to boot!* Heaven help me!   ⁸¹ *make no conclusion*
don't pursue that line of argument

Leontes.   Never but once.

Hermione. What! Have I twice said well? When was 't
    before?   90
  I prithee tell me; cram 's with praise, and make 's
  As fat as tame things: one good deed, dying tongue-
      less,
  Slaughters a thousand waiting upon that.
  Our praises are our wages—you may ride's
  With one soft kiss a thousand furlongs, ere   95
  With spur we heat an acre.° But to th' goal:
  My last good deed was to entreat his stay.
  What was my first? It has an elder sister,
  Or I mistake you; O, would her name were Grace!
  But once before I spoke to th' purpose? When?   100
  Nay, let me have 't; I long.

Leontes.   Why, that was when
  Three crabbèd months had soured themselves to
      death,
  Ere I could make thee open thy white hand
  And clap° thyself my love; then didst thou utter
  "I am yours forever."

Hermione.   'Tis Grace indeed.   105
  Why, lo you now, I have spoke to th' purpose twice:
  The one forever earned a royal husband;
  Th' other, for some while a friend.

Leontes.   [*Aside*] Too hot, too hot!
  To mingle friendship far is mingling bloods.
  I have tremor cordis° on me; my heart dances,   110
  But not for joy, not joy. This entertainment
  May a free face put on, derive a liberty
  From heartiness, from bounty, fertile bosom,°
  And well become the agent—'t may, I grant;
  But to be paddling palms and pinching fingers,   115
  As now they are, and making practiced smiles
  As in a looking glass; and then to sigh, as 'twere

---

⁹⁶ *heat an acre* race over a furlong ¹⁰⁴ *clap* offer the handclasp that
seals a bargain ¹¹⁰ *tremor cordis* palpitation of the heart ¹¹³ *fertile
bosom* generous affection

The mort o' th' deer° —oh, that is entertainment
My bosom likes not, nor my brows.° Mamillius,
Art thou my boy?

Mamillius.   Ay, my good lord.

120 *Leontes.*   I' fecks!°
Why, that's my bawcock.° What, hast smutched thy
     nose?
They say it is a copy out of mine. Come, Captain,
We must be neat—not neat,° but cleanly, Captain:
And yet the steer, the heifer, and the calf,
125 Are all called neat. Still virginaling°
Upon his palm? How now, you wanton calf,
Art thou my calf?

Mamillius.   Yes, if you will, my lord.

Leontes. Thou want'st a rough pash,° and the shoots
     that I have
To be full like me: yet they say we are
130 Almost as like as eggs; women say so,
That will say anything. But were they false
As o'er-dyed blacks,° as wind, as waters; false
As dice are to be wished, by one that fixes
No bourn° 'twixt his and mine—yet were it true
135 To say this boy were like me. Come, Sir Page,
Look on me with your welkin° eye. Sweet villain,
Most dear'st, my collop!° Can thy dam,° may 't be?
Affection!° Thy intention° stabs the center.°
Thou dost make possible things not so held,
140 Communicat'st with dreams—how can this be?—
With what's unreal thou coactive art,

117-18 *as 'twere/The mort o' th' deer* like the horn call signifying the
death of the deer 119 *brows* (alluding to the myth of the horns that
grow on the foreheads of cuckolds) 120 *fecks* (a mild oath, derived
from "i' faith") 121 *bawcock* fine fellow (Fr. *beau coq*) 123 *neat*
(Leontes rejects the word because it also means "horned cattle")
125 *virginaling* i.e., as if playing the virginals (a small keyboard instrument) 128 *pash* head 132 *o'er-dyed blacks* black garments worn out
by too much dyeing 134 *bourn* boundary 136 *welkin* blue (like the sky)
137 *collop* a cut off his own flesh 137 *dam* mother (Leontes' thoughts
still run on cattle) 138 *Affection* passion 138 *intention* purpose
138 *center* i.e., of the world (?) of my heart (?)

And fellow'st nothing. Then 'tis very credent°
Thou mayst co-join with something, and thou dost,
And that beyond commission, and I find it,
And that to the infection of my brains,   145
And hardening of my brows.°

Polixenes.   What means Sicilia?

Hermione. He something seems unsettled.

Polixenes.   How, my lord?

Leontes. What cheer? How is 't with you, best brother?

Hermione.   You look
As if you held a brow of much distraction;
Are you moved, my lord?

Leontes.   No, in good earnest.   150
How sometimes Nature will betray its folly,
Its tenderness, and make itself a pastime
To harder bosoms! Looking on the lines
Of my boy's face, methoughts I did recoil
Twenty-three years, and saw myself unbreeched,   155
In my green velvet coat; my dagger muzzled,
Lest it should bite its master, and so prove,
As ornaments oft do, too dangerous.
How like, methought, I then was to this kernel,
This squash,° this gentleman. Mine honest friend,   160
Will you take eggs for money?°

Mamillius. No, my lord, I'll fight.

Leontes. You will? Why, happy man be 's dole!° My
    brother,

---

¹⁴² *credent* credible   ¹³⁸⁻⁴⁶ *Affection . . . brows* (may be corrupt.
Paraphrase: "Passion! Your desire for fulfillment can pierce to the heart
of things. You deal with matters normally thought of as illusory—with
dreams and fantasies, impossible as that sounds. You collaborate with
the unreal; so it isn't improbable that you should do so with what
really exists; this is what has happened, as my mental disturbance and
cuckold's horns indicate." The passion is jealousy; Leontes recognizes
that it is sometimes baseless, but argues that it is not so in his case)
¹⁶⁰ *squash* unripe peapod (young person)   ¹⁶¹ *take eggs for money*
allow yourself to be imposed upon   ¹⁶³ *happy man be 's dole* may it be
his lot to be a happy man

Are you so fond of your young prince as we
Do seem to be of ours?

165 *Polixenes.*   If at home, sir,
He's all my exercise, my mirth, my matter;
Now my sworn friend, and then mine enemy;
My parasite, my soldier, statesman, all.
He makes a July's day short as December,
170 And with his varying childness, cures in me
Thoughts that would thick my blood.°

Leontes.   So stands this squire
Officed with me.° We two will walk, my lord,
And leave you to your graver steps. Hermione,
How thou lov'st us, show in our brother's welcome;
175 Let what is dear in Sicily, be cheap;
Next to thyself and my young rover, he's
Apparent° to my heart.

Hermione.   If you would seek us,
We are yours i' th' garden; shall's attend you there?

Leontes. To your own bents dispose you; you'll be
found,
180 Be you beneath the sky. [*Aside*] I am angling° now,
Though you perceive me not how I give line.
Go to, go to!
How she holds up the neb,° the bill to him!
And arms her with the boldness of a wife
To her allowing° husband!

            [*Exeunt Polixenes, Hermione, and Attendants.*]
185   Gone already!
Inch-thick, knee-deep, o'er head and ears a forked°
one!
Go play, boy, play: thy mother plays, and I
Play too—but so disgraced a part, whose issue°
Will hiss me to my grave; contempt and clamor

---

¹⁷¹ *thick my blood* make me melancholy   ¹⁷¹⁻⁷² *So stands . . . me* My
son has a similar post in my household   ¹⁷⁷ *Apparent* heir apparent
¹⁸⁰ *angling* giving them scope, "playing" them   ¹⁸³ *neb* beak   ¹⁸⁵ *allowing* approving   ¹⁸⁶ *forked* (alluding to the branching cuckold's
horns)   ¹⁸⁸ *issue* exit (following the idea of the actor not capable of
his part)

Will be my knell. Go play, boy, play. There have
    been,   190
Or I am much deceived, cuckolds ere now,
And many a man there is, even at this present,
Now, while I speak this, holds his wife by th' arm,
That little thinks she has been sluiced in 's absence,
And his pond fished by his next neighbor, by   195
Sir Smile, his neighbor, nay, there's comfort in 't,
Whiles other men have gates, and those gates
    opened,
As mine, against their will. Should all despair,
That have revolted° wives, the tenth of mankind
Would hang themselves. Physic for 't there's none;   200
It is a bawdy planet, that will strike
Where 'tis predominant;° and 'tis powerful, think it,
From east, west, north, and south. Be it concluded,
No barricado for a belly. Know 't
It will let in and out the enemy,   205
With bag and baggage. Many thousand on 's
Have the disease, and feel 't not. How now, boy!

Mamillius. I am like you, they say.

Leontes.   Why, that's some comfort.
What! Camillo there?

Camillo. Ay, my good lord.   210

Leontes. Go play, Mamillius; thou 'rt an honest man.

                              [*Exit Mamillius.*]

    Camillo, this great sir will yet stay longer.

Camillo. You had much ado to make his anchor hold;
When you cast out, it still came home.

Leontes.   Didst note it?

Camillo. He would not stay at your petitions, made   215
His business more material.

Leontes.   Didst perceive it?

199 *revolted* unfaithful   202 *predominant* in the ascendant (a technical
term in astrology)

[*Aside*] They're here° with me already: whispering,
    rounding:°
"Sicilia is a so-forth":° 'tis far gone,
When I shall gust° it last. How came 't, Camillo,
That he did stay?

220 *Camillo.*   At the good Queen's entreaty.

Leontes. "At the Queen's" be 't: "Good" should be
    pertinent,
But so it is, it is not. Was this taken°
By any understanding pate but thine?
For thy conceit is soaking,° will draw in
225 More than the common blocks.° Not noted, is 't,
But of the finer natures? By some severals°
Of headpiece extraordinary? Lower messes°
Perchance are to this business purblind? Say.

Camillo. Business, my lord? I think most understand
Bohemia stays here longer.

Leontes.   Ha?

230 *Camillo.*   Stays here longer.

Leontes. Ay, but why?

Camillo. To satisfy your Highness, and the entreaties
Of our most gracious mistress.

Leontes.   Satisfy
Th' entreaties of your mistress? Satisfy?
235 Let that suffice. I have trusted thee, Camillo,
With all the nearest things to my heart, as well
My chamber-counsels,° wherein, priestlike, thou
Hast cleansed my bosom—ay, from thee departed
Thy penitent reformed; but we have been
240 Deceived in thy integrity, deceived
In that which seems so.

217 *They're here* They (onlookers) have already caught on to my situation   217 *rounding* speaking in secret   218 *so-forth* i.e., they slyly avoid
the word "cuckold"   219 *gust* taste, hear of   222 *taken* observed
224 *conceit is soaking* intelligence is absorbent   225 *blocks* blockheads
226 *severals* individuals   227 *Lower messes* inferior people ("mess" in the
sense of a group who dine together and would be of the same—low—
rank)   237 *chamber-counsels* confessions of secret sins

Camillo.   Be it forbid, my lord!

Leontes. To bide° upon 't. Thou art not honest; or
　If thou inclin'st that way, thou art a coward,
　Which hoxes° honesty behind, restraining
　From course required; or else thou must be counted   245
　A servant, grafted in my serious trust,
　And therein negligent; or else a fool,
　That seest a game played home, the rich stake
　　drawn,°
　And tak'st it all for jest.

Camillo.   My gracious lord,
　I may be negligent, foolish, and fearful,   250
　In every one of these no man is free
　But that his negligence, his folly, fear,
　Among the infinite doings of the world,
　Sometime puts forth.° In your affairs, my lord,
　If ever I were willful negligent,   255
　It was my folly; if industriously
　I played the fool, it was my negligence,
　Not weighing well the end: if ever fearful
　To do a thing, where I the issue doubted,
　Whereof the execution did cry out   260
　Against the nonperformance, 'twas a fear
　Which oft infects the wisest. These, my lord,
　Are such allowed infirmities, that honesty
　Is never free of. But beseech your Grace,
　Be plainer with me, let me know my trespass   265
　By its own visage;° if I then deny it,
　'Tis none of mine.

Leontes.   Ha' not you seen, Camillo—
　But that's past doubt, you have, or your eyeglass°
　Is thicker than a cuckold's horn—or heard—
　For to a vision so apparent, rumor   270
　Cannot be mute—or thought—for cogitation
　Resides not in that man that does not think—

---

²⁴² *bide* insist ²⁴⁴ *hoxes* hamstrings ²⁴⁸ *played home . . . stake drawn*
played earnestly, great stakes being won ²⁵⁴ *puts forth* shows itself
²⁶⁶ *by its own visage* under its true name ²⁶⁸ *eyeglass* the lens of the
eye

My wife is slippery?° If thou wilt confess,
Or else be impudently negative,
275   To have nor eyes, nor ears, nor thought, then say
My wife's a hobbyhorse,° deserves a name
As rank as any flax-wench,° that puts to
Before her troth-plight; say 't, and justify 't.

Camillo. I would not be a stander-by to hear
280   My sovereign mistress clouded so, without
My present° vengeance taken; 'shrew my heart,
You never spoke what did become you less
Than this; which to reiterate, were sin
As deep as that, though true.°

Leontes.   Is whispering nothing?
285   Is leaning cheek to cheek? Is meeting noses?
Kissing with inside lip? Stopping the career°
Of laughter with a sigh (a note infallible
Of breaking honesty°)? Horsing foot on foot?
Skulking in corners? Wishing clocks more swift?
290   Hours, minutes? Noon, midnight? And all eyes
Blind with the pin and web,° but theirs; theirs only,
That would unseen be wicked? Is this nothing?
Why, then the world and all that's in 't is nothing,
The covering sky is nothing, Bohemia nothing,
295   My wife is nothing, nor nothing have these nothings,
If this be nothing.

Camillo.   Good my lord, be cured
Of this diseased opinion, and betimes,
For 'tis most dangerous.

Leontes.   Say it be, 'tis true.

Camillo. No, no, my lord.

Leontes.   It is; you lie, you lie.

---

²⁶⁷⁻⁷³ *Ha' not you . . . slippery?* Have you not seen—you must have,
or your sight is grossly thick—or heard—as you must, since Hermione's
conduct is so open that there must be gossip about it—or thought—
and unless you have you can't think at all—that my wife is unfaithful?
²⁷⁶ *hobbyhorse* loose woman   ²⁷⁷ *flax-wench* low-bred girl   ²⁸¹ *present*
immediate   ²⁸⁴ *As deep as that, though true* i.e., as wicked as her adultery if it were a fact, which it is not   ²⁸⁶ *career* gallop   ²⁸⁸ *honesty*
chastity   ²⁹¹ *pin and web* cataract

I say thou liest, Camillo, and I hate thee,   *800*
Pronounce thee a gross lout, a mindless slave,
Or else a hovering° temporizer, that
Canst with thine eyes at once see good and evil,
Inclining to them both. Were my wife's liver°
Infected as her life, she would not live   *805*
The running of one glass.°

Camillo.   Who does infect her?

Leontes. Why, he that wears her like her medal,°
  hanging
About his neck, Bohemia, who, if I
Had servants true about me, that bare eyes
To see alike mine honor as their profits,   *810*
Their own particular thrifts,° they would do that
Which should undo more doing. Ay, and thou,
His cupbearer, whom I from meaner form
Have benched° and reared to worship, who mayst
  see
Plainly as heaven sees earth, and earth see heaven, *815*
How I am gallèd, mightst bespice a cup,
To give mine enemy a lasting wink;°
Which draught to me were cordial.°

Camillo.   Sir, my lord,
I could do this, and that with no rash potion,
But with a lingering dram° that should not work   *820*
Maliciously, like poison; but I cannot
Believe this crack to be in my dread mistress,
So sovereignly being honorable.
I have loved thee————°

Leontes. Make that thy question, and go rot!°   *825*

302 *hovering* vacillating 304 *liver* (since this was the seat of the passions, it presumably was infected; transposition of "liver" and "life" has
been proposed) 306 *glass* hourglass 307 *medal* (here a portrait minia-
ture worn about the neck) 311 *particular* thrifts special gains 314
benched i.e., raised to place of dignity 317 *give . . . lasting wink*,
i.e., close his eyes forever 318 *cordial* medicine 320 *lingering dram*
slow-working dose 324 *I have loved thee* (difficult to explain: Camillo
may be about to protest his long loyalty, or threaten withdrawal of his
love, but he would hardly address the King as "thou." Some editors
give the words to Leontes, which hardly helps) 325 *Make . . . rot* i.e.,
if you doubt the Queen's infidelity, go to hell

Dost think I am so muddy, so unsettled,
To appoint° myself in this vexation? Sully
The purity and whiteness of my sheets—
Which to preserve is sleep; which being spotted,
330 Is goads, thorns, nettles, tails of wasps—
Give scandal to the blood o' th' prince, my son,
Who I do think is mine, and love as mine,
Without ripe° moving to 't? Would I do this?
Could man so blench?°

Camillo.   I must believe you, sir;
335 I do, and will fetch off Bohemia for 't:
Provided that when he's removed, your Highness
Will take again your queen as yours at first,
Even for your son's sake, and thereby for sealing
The injury of tongues, in courts and kingdoms
Known and allied to yours.

340 *Leontes.*   Thou dost advise me,
Even so as I mine own course have set down.
I'll give no blemish to her honor, none.

Camillo. My lord,
Go then; and with a countenance as clear
345 As friendship wears at feasts, keep with Bohemia,
And with your queen: I am his cupbearer;
If from me he have wholesome beverage,
Account me not your servant.

Leontes.   This is all:
Do 't, and thou hast the one half of my heart;
Do 't not, thou split'st thine own.

350 *Camillo.*   I'll do 't, my lord.

Leontes. I will seem friendly, as thou hast advised me.

                                        Exit.

Camillo. O miserable lady! But for me,
What case stand I in? I must be the poisoner
Of good Polixenes, and my ground to do 't
355 Is the obedience to a master—one
Who, in rebellion with himself, will have
All that are his so too. To do this deed,

327 *appoint* establish   333 *ripe* adequate, matured   334 *blench* swerve

Promotion follows; if I could find example
Of thousands that had struck anointed kings,
And flourished after, I'd not do 't; but since   360
Nor brass, nor stone, nor parchment bears not one,
Let villainy itself forswear 't.° I must
Forsake the court; to do 't, or no, is certain
To me a break-neck. Happy star reign now!
Here comes Bohemia.

Enter Polixenes.

Polixenes.   This is strange: methinks   865
My favor here begins to warp. Not speak?
Good day, Camillo.

Camillo.   Hail, most royal sir.

Polixenes. What is the news i' th' court?

Camillo.   None rare, my lord.

Polixenes. The King hath on him such a countenance,
As he had lost some province, and a region   870
Loved as he loves himself; even now I met him
With customary compliment, when he,
Wafting his eyes to th' contrary,° and falling
A lip of much contempt, speed from me, and
So leaves me to consider what is breeding   875
That changes thus his manners.

Camillo. I dare not know, my lord.

Polixenes. How, dare not? Do not? Do you know, and
      dare not
Be intelligent to me? 'Tis thereabouts;
For to yourself, what you do know, you must,   880
And cannot say you dare not.° Good Camillo,
Your changed complexions are to me a mirror,
Which shows me mine changed too: for I must be
A party in this alteration, finding

858–62 *if I could example . . . forswear 't* if the records showed that king-killers prospered, I would not do it; but since they prove the contrary, villainy itself should forswear regicide 373 *Wafting his eyes to th' contrary* looking (contemptuously) away 378–81 *How, dare not? . . . you dare not* What do you mean, dare not? That you do not? Can it be that you know, and dare not tell me? That must be the explanation, since you can't say you don't dare tell yourself what you know

                Myself thus altered with 't.
385 *Camillo.*   There is a sickness
                Which puts some of us in distemper; but
                I cannot name the disease; and it is caught
                Of you, that yet are well.

     Polixenes.   How caught of me?
                Make me not sighted like the basilisk.°
                I have looked on thousands, who have sped° the
890   better
                By my regard, but killed none so. Camillo,
                As you are certainly a gentleman, thereto
                Clerklike experienced,° which no less adorns
                Our gentry than our parents' noble names
395   In whose success° we are gentle:° I beseech you,
                If you know aught which does behoove my knowledge
                Thereof to be informed, imprison 't not
                In ignorant concealment.

     Camillo.   I may not answer.

     Polixenes. A sickness caught of me, and yet I well?
400   I must be answered. Dost thou hear, Camillo,
                I conjure° thee, by all the parts° of man,
                Which honor does acknowledge, whereof the least
                Is not this suit of mine, that thou declare
                What incidency° thou dost guess of harm
405   Is creeping toward me; how far off, how near,
                Which way to be prevented, if to be;
                If not, how best to bear it.

     Camillo.   Sir, I will tell you,
                Since I am charged in honor, and by him
                That I think honorable. Therefore mark my counsel,
410   Which must be ev'n as swiftly followed as
                I mean to utter it; or both yourself and me,
                Cry lost, and so good night.

     Polixenes.   On, good Camillo.

     Camillo. I am appointed him° to murder you.

---

889 *basilisk* a mythical serpent which killed by looking   890 *sped* prospered   398 *Clerklike experienced* with the experience of an educated
man   395 *success* succession   395 *gentle* well born   401 *conjure* adjure
401 *parts* duties, functions   404 *incidency* threat   418 *him* i.e., by Leontes

Polixenes. By whom, Camillo?

Camillo.   By the King.

Polixenes.   For what?

Camillo. He thinks, nay with all confidence he swears,   415
As he had seen 't, or been an instrument
To vice° you to 't, that you have touched his queen
Forbiddenly.

Polixenes.   Oh then my best blood turn
To an infected jelly, and my name
Be yoked with his, that did betray the Best!°   420
Turn then my freshest reputation to
A savor° that may strike the dullest nostril
Where I arrive, and my approach be shunned,
Nay, hated too, worse than the great'st infection
That e'er was heard, or read!

Camillo.   Swear his thought over°   425
By each particular star in heaven, and
By all their influences; you may as well
Forbid the sea for to obey the moon,
As or by oath remove or counsel shake
The fabric of his folly, whose foundation   430
Is piled upon his faith, and will continue
The standing of his body.°

Polixenes.   How should this grow?°

Camillo. I know not: but I am sure 'tis safer to
Avoid what's grown than question how 'tis born.
If therefore you dare trust my honesty,   435
That lies enclosèd in this trunk, which you
Shall bear along impawned,° away tonight.
Your followers I will whisper to the business,

---

⁴¹⁷ *To vice* to force   ⁴²⁰ *his, that did betray the Best* i.e., Judas
⁴²² *savor* alluding to the idea that infection (e.g., of the plague) could be
smelled (hence the use of flowers in posies as a prophylactic)   ⁴²⁵ *Swear
his thought over* deny his suspicion with oaths   ⁴²⁹⁻³² *As or by oath
. . . of his body* i.e., you may as well attempt the obviously impossible
as try to remove by your oaths or pull down by your advice the structure of his crazy delusion which has its foundations on settled belief,
and will last as long as his life (stand up as long as he can)   ⁴³² *How
should this grow?* How can this have grown up   ⁴³⁷ *impawned* as a
pledge of good faith (Camillo points to his body, which is the "trunk")

          And will by twos and threes, at several posterns,°
440   Clear them o' th' city. For myself, I'll put
          My fortunes to your service, which are here
          By this discovery lost. Be not uncertain,
          For by the honor of my parents, I
          Have uttered truth; which if you seek to prove,°
445   I dare not stand by; nor shall you be safer,
          Than one condemned by the King's own mouth,
                    thereon
          His execution sworn.°

Polixenes.   I do believe thee:
          I saw his heart in 's face. Give me thy hand,
          Be pilot to me, and thy places° shall
450   Still neighbor mine. My ships are ready, and
          My people did expect my hence departure
          Two days ago. This jealousy
          Is for a precious creature; as she's rare,
          Must it be great; and, as his person's mighty,
455   Must it be violent: and, as he does conceive,
          He is dishonored by a man, which ever
          Professed° to him, why his revenges must
          In that be made more bitter. Fear o'ershades me;
          Good expedition° by my friend, and comfort
460   The gracious Queen, part of his theme, but nothing
          Of his ill-ta'en suspicion.° Come, Camillo,
          I will respect thee as a father, if
          Thou bear'st my life off hence; let us avoid.°

Camillo. It is in mine authority to command
465   The keys of all the posterns: please your Highness
          To take the urgent hour. Come, sir, away.   *Exeunt.*

⁴³⁹ *posterns* gates   ⁴⁴⁴ *prove* test   ⁴⁴⁶⁻⁴⁷ *mouth . . . sworn* i.e., the
King having condemned him has sworn that the sentence will be death
(Corrupt? See list of emendations.)   ⁴⁴⁹ *places* offices, functions, dignities   ⁴⁵⁷ *Professed* made professions (of friendship)   ⁴⁵⁹ *expedition*
speed   ⁴⁶⁰⁻⁶¹ *part of his theme . . . suspicion* (obscure: Shakespeare's
sense has perhaps not quite got through. "May my speedy departure
also help the Queen, who is involved in Leontes' fantasy though she
has no rightful place in his suspicions." But this fails to explain why
Polixenes thought his departure would help Hermione. Perhaps "expedition" is not the subject of "comfort"—then he is merely wishing the
Queen comfort in the troubles he is leaving her to, and the vagueness
of the expression matches the emptiness of the wish).   ⁴⁶³ *avoid* depart

ACT II

Scene I. [*Sicilia, the Court of Leontes.*]

Enter Hermione, Mamillius, Ladies.

Hermione. Take the boy to you; he so troubles me,
  'Tis past enduring.

First Lady   Come, my gracious lord,
  Shall I be your playfellow?

Mamillius.   No, I'll none of you.

First Lady. Why, my sweet lord?

Mamillius. You'll kiss me hard, and speak to me, as if   5
  I were a baby still. I love you better.

Second Lady. And why so, my lord?

Mamillius.   Not for because
  Your brows are blacker; yet black brows, they say,
  Become some women best, so that there be not
  Too much hair there, but in a semicircle,   10
  Or a half-moon, made with a pen.

Second Lady.   Who taught'° this?

Mamillius. I learned it out of women's faces. Pray now,
  What color are your eyebrows?

First Lady.   Blue, my lord.

II.i.[11] *taught'* taught you

59

Mamillius. Nay, that's a mock. I have seen a lady's
    nose
    That has been blue, but not her eyebrows.

15 *First Lady.*   Hark ye,
    The Queen, your mother, rounds apace; we shall
    Present our services to a fine new prince
    One of these days, and then you'd wanton° with us,
    If we would have you.

Second Lady.   She is spread of late
20   Into a goodly bulk; good time encounter her!

Hermione. What wisdom stirs amongst you? Come, sir,
    now
    I am for you again; pray you sit by us,
    And tell 's a tale.

Mamillius.   Merry or sad shall 't be?

Hermione. As merry as you will.

25 *Mamillius.* A sad tale's best for winter; I have one
    Of sprites and goblins.

Hermione.   Let's have that, good sir.
    Come on, sit down; come on, and do your best,
    To fright me with your sprites; you're powerful at it.

Mamillius. There was a man.

Hermione.   Nay, come sit down; then on.

30 *Mamillius.* Dwelt by a churchyard—I will tell it softly,
    Yond crickets° shall not hear it.

Hermione. Come on, then, and give 't me in mine ear.

    [*Enter Leontes, Antigonus, and Lords.*]

Leontes. Was he met there? His train? Camillo with
    him?

Lord. Behind the tuft of pines I met them, never
35   Saw I men scour° so on their way. I eyed them
    Even to their ships.

Leontes.   How blest am I

---

18 *wanton* play   31 *yond crickets* i.e., the chattering ladies   35 *scour*
hurry

In my just censure,° in my true opinion!
Alack, for lesser knowledge! How accursed,
In being so blest! There may be in the cup
A spider° steeped, and one may drink, depart,   40
And yet partake no venom, for his knowledge
Is not infected; but if one present
Th' abhorred ingredient to his eye, make known
How he hath drunk, he cracks his gorge, his sides,
With violent hefts.° I have drunk, and seen the
          spider.   45
Camillo was his help in this, his pander.
There is a plot against my life, my crown;
All's true that is mistrusted; that false villain,
Whom I employed, was pre-employed by him;
He has discovered° my design, and I   50
Remain a pinched thing;° yea, a very trick
For them to play at will. How came the posterns
So easily open?

Lord.   By his great authority;
Which often hath no less prevailed than so
On your command.

Leontes.   I know 't too well.   55
    [*To Hermione*] Give me the boy. I am glad you did
          not nurse him;
    Though he does bear some signs of me, yet you
    Have too much blood in him.

Hermione.   What is this? Sport?

Leontes. Bear the boy hence, he shall not come about
          her;

                    [*Exit Mamillius and a Lady.*]
    Away with him, and let her sport herself
    With that she's big with; for 'tis Polixenes   60
    Has made thee swell thus.

Hermione.   But I'd say he had not;

---

³⁷ *censure* judgment   ⁴⁰ *spider* (spiders were thought of as venomous; there seems to have been a superstition that this was so only if one saw the spider)   ⁴⁵ *hefts* retchings   ⁵⁰ *discovered* revealed   ⁵¹ *pinched thing* puppet, toy

And I'll be sworn you would believe my saying,
Howe'er you lean to th' nayward.°

Leontes.   You, my lords,
65 Look on her, mark her well; be but about
To say, "She is a goodly lady," and
The justice of your hearts will thereto add,
" 'Tis pity she's not honest, honorable";
Praise her but for this her without-door form,°
70 Which on my faith deserves high speech, and straight
The shrug, the hum or ha, these petty brands
That calumny doth use—oh, I am out!°
That mercy does, for calumny will sear
Virtue itself—these shrugs, these hum's and ha's,
75 When you have said she's goodly, come between,°
Ere you can say she's honest. But be 't known,
From him that has most cause to grieve it should be,
She's an adult'ress.

Hermione.   Should a villain say so,
The most replenished° villain in the world,
80 He were as much more villain; you, my lord,
Do but mistake.

Leontes.   You have mistook, my lady,
Polixenes for Leontes. O thou thing,
Which I'll not call a creature of thy place,°
Lest barbarism, making me the precedent,
85 Should a like language use to all degrees,°
And mannerly distinguishment leave out
Betwixt the prince and beggar. I have said
She's an adult'ress, I have said with whom.
More, she's a traitor, and Camillo is
90 A federary° with her, and one that knows
What she should shame to know herself
But with her most vile principal° —that she's
A bed-swerver,° even as bad as those

---

⁶⁴ *nayward* negative ⁶⁹ *without-door form* external appearance ⁷² *I am out* I have lost my place, got my speech wrong ⁷⁵ *come between* pause, interrupt, break off ⁷⁹ *replenished* complete, perfect ⁸³ *place* rank   ⁸⁵ *degrees* social ranks ⁹⁰ *federary* confederate, accomplice ⁹² *principal* partner (i.e., Polixenes) ⁹³ *bed-swerver* adulteress

That vulgars give bold'st titles; ay, and privy
To this their late escape.

Hermione.   No, by my life,   95
  Privy to none of this; how will this grieve you,
  When you shall come to clearer knowledge, that
  You thus have published° me! Gentle my lord,
  You scarce can right me throughly then to say
  You did mistake.

Leontes.   No; if I mistake   100
  In those foundations which I build upon,
  The center° is not big enough to bear
  A schoolboy's top. Away with her to prison.
  He who shall speak for her is afar off guilty,
  But that he speaks.°

Hermione.   There's some ill planet reigns;   105
  I must be patient, till the heavens look
  With an aspect more favorable. Good my lords,
  I am not prone to weeping, as our sex
  Commonly are; the want of which vain dew
  Perchance shall dry your pities. But I have   110
  That honorable grief lodged here which burns
  Worse than tears drown. Beseech you all, my lords,
  With thoughts so qualified° as your charities
  Shall best instruct you, measure me; and so
  The King's will be performed!

Leontes.   Shall I be heard?   115

Hermione. Who is 't that goes with me? Beseech your
    Highness
  My women may be with me, for you see
  My plight requires it. Do not weep, good fools;
  There is no cause; when you shall know your mis-
    tress
  Has deserved prison, then abound in tears,   120
  As I come out; this action I now go on

---

⁹⁸ *published* publicly proclaimed or denounced ¹⁰² *center* (of the
earth, and so of the universe), i.e., "If I am mistaken, no foundation
can be trusted" ¹⁰⁵ *But that he speaks* i.e., in merely speaking he is
found guilty as a remote accomplice ¹¹³ *qualified* tempered, moderated

Is for my better grace.° Adieu, my lord.
I never wished to see you sorry; now
I trust I shall. My women come, you have leave.

125 *Leontes.* Go, do our bidding: hence.

[*Exeunt Queen and Ladies.*]

Lord. Beseech your Highness, call the Queen again.

Antigonus. Be certain what you do, sir, lest your justice
   Prove violence, in the which three great ones suffer,
   Yourself, your queen, your son.

Lord.   For her, my lord,
130 I dare my life lay down, and will do 't, sir,
   Please you t' accept it, that the Queen is spotless
   I' th' eyes of heaven, and to you—I mean,
   In this, which you accuse her.

Antigonus.   If it prove
   She's otherwise, I'll keep my stables where
135 I lodge my wife;° I'll go in couples° with her;
   Than when I feel and see her, no farther trust her;
   For every inch of woman in the world,
   Ay, every dram of woman's flesh is false,
   If she be.

Leontes. Hold your peaces.

Lord.   Good my lord.

140 *Antigonus.* It is for you we speak, not for ourselves.
   You are abused, and by some putter-on°
   That will be damned for 't. Would I knew the villain,
   I would land-damn° him! Be she honor-flawed,
   I have three daughters: the eldest is eleven;
145 The second and the third, nine and some five:
   If this prove true, they'll pay for 't. By mine honor,

121-22 *this action . . . grace* by contrast with one who goes to prison
to be disgraced, I embark on this course to add to my honesty and
credit   134-35 *I'll keep my stables . . . wife* (obscure but certainly
coarse. He will keep his stallions locked up when his wife is near?)
135 *go in couples* be coupled by a leash to her, for safety's sake (of
course, he means that if the Queen is unchaste, other women must be
even more so)   141 *putter-on* plotter, one who instigates   143 *land-damn*
severely beat (?)

I'll geld 'em all; fourteen they shall not see
To bring false generations.° They are co-heirs,
And I had rather glib° myself than they
Should not produce fair issue.

Leontes.   Cease, no more!   150
You smell this business with a sense as cold
As is a dead man's nose; but I do see 't, and feel 't,
As you feel doing thus; and see withal
The instruments that feel.°

Antigonus.   If it be so,
We need no grave to bury honesty;   155
There's not a grain of it the face to sweeten
Of the whole dungy earth.

Leontes.   What? Lack I credit?°

Lord. I had rather you did lack than I, my lord,
Upon this ground; and more it would content me
To have her honor true than your suspicion,   160
Be blamed for 't how you might.

Leontes.   Why, what need we
Commune with you of this, but rather follow
Our forceful instigation? Our prerogative
Calls not your counsels, but our natural goodness
Imparts this;° which, if you, or stupefied,   165
Or seeming so, in skill,° cannot, or will not,
Relish a truth like us, inform yourselves,
We need no more of your advice. The matter,
The loss, the gain, the ord'ring on 't,
Is all properly ours.

Antigonus.   And I wish, my liege,   170
You had only in your silent judgment tried it,
Without more overture.

---

[148] *false generations* illegitimate children   [149] *glib* castrate   [152-54] *but I do see . . . that feel* (Leontes here strikes either Antigonus or himself. "But I see it and feel it with immediate, vital force, as you do when you strike yourself thus [or, when I strike you thus]—you feel it and see the hands that inflicted the pain")   [157] *Lack I credit?* am I not believed   [163-65] *Our prerogative . . . imparts this* i.e., I'm not obliged to seek your advice; it's out of the goodness of my heart that I tell you this (Leontes, on his dignity, uses the royal "we")   [166] *skill* reason

Leontes.   How could that be?
 Either thou art most ignorant by age,
 Or thou wert born a fool. Camillo's flight,
175 Added to their familiarity—
 Which was as gross as ever touched conjecture,°
 That lacked sight only, naught for approbation°
 But only seeing, all other circumstances
 Made up to th' deed—doth push on this proceeding.
180 Yet, for a greater confirmation—
 For in an act of this importance, 'twere
 Most piteous to be wild° —I have dispatched in post
 To sacred Delphos,° to Apollo's temple,
 Cleomenes and Dion, whom you know
185 Of stuffed sufficiency.° Now, from the oracle
 They will bring all,° whose spiritual counsel had,
 Shall stop, or spur me. Have I done well?

Lord. Well done, my lord.

Leontes. Though I am satisfied, and need no more
190 Than what I know, yet shall the oracle
 Give rest to th' minds of others—such as he,°
 Whose ignorant credulity will not
 Come up to th' truth. So have we thought it good
 From our free person she should be confined,
195 Lest that the treachery of the two fled hence
 Be left her to perform.° Come, follow us,
 We are to speak in public: for this business
 Will raise° us all.

Antigonus.   [*Aside*] To laughter, as I take it,
 If the good truth were known.   *Exeunt.*

---

176 *as ever touched conjecture* as ever conjecture reached to   177 *approbation* proof   182 *wild* rash   183 *Delphos* Delos (Shakespeare mistakenly thought the oracle of Apollo was there rather than at Delphi. In this error he follows his source, *Pandosto*)   185 *stuffed sufficiency* more than adequate dependability   186 *all* the whole truth   191 *such as he* i.e., Antigonus   195–96 *Lest that . . . perform* (referring to the "plot against his life and crown" of which he accuses all three)   198 *raise* rouse

Scene II. [*Sicilia, a prison.*]

Enter Paulina, a Gentleman, [and Attendants].

Paulina. The keeper of the prison, call to him;
Let him have knowledge who I am.

                              [*Exit Gentleman.*]
                    Good lady,
No court in Europe is too good for thee—
What dost thou then in prison?

          [*Enter Gentleman with the*] Jailer.

                         Now, good sir,
You know me, do you not?

Jailer.   For a worthy lady,   5
And one whom much I honor.

Paulina.   Pray you, then,
Conduct me to the Queen.

Jailer.   I may not, madam,
To the contrary I have express commandment.

Paulina. Here's ado, to lock up honesty and honor
     from
Th' access of gentle visitors! Is 't lawful, pray you,   10
To see her women? Any of them? Emilia?

Jailer. So please you, madam,
To put apart these your attendants, I
Shall bring Emilia forth.

Paulina.   I pray now call her.
Withdraw yourselves.

               [*Exit Gentleman and Attendants.*]
Jailer.   And, madam,
I must be present at your conference.   15

Paulina. Well, be 't so, prithee.   [*Exit Jailer.*]
 Here's such ado to make no stain a stain,
 As passes coloring.°

     [*Enter Jailer, with*] *Emilia.*

        Dear gentlewoman,
20 How fares our gracious lady?

Emilia. As well as one so great and so forlorn
 May hold together. On her frights and griefs
 (Which° never tender lady hath borne greater)
 She is, something before her time, delivered.

Paulina. A boy?

25 *Emilia.*   A daughter, and a goodly babe,
 Lusty, and like to live; the Queen receives
 Much comfort in 't; says, "My poor prisoner,
 I am innocent as you."

Paulina.   I dare be sworn.
 These dangerous, unsafe lunes° i' th' King, beshrew
  them!
30 He must be told on 't, and he shall; the office
 Becomes a woman best. I'll take 't upon me.
 If I prove honey-mouthed, let my tongue blister,°
 And never to my red-looked anger be
 The trumpet° any more. Pray you, Emilia,
35 Commend my best obedience to the Queen;
 If she dares trust me with her little babe,
 I'll show 't the King, and undertake to be
 Her advocate to th' loud'st. We do not know
 How he may soften at the sight o' th' child;
40 The silence often of pure innocence
 Persuades, when speaking fails.

Emilia.   Most worthy madam,
 Your honor and your goodness is so evident,

II.ii.[19] *coloring* the art of dyeing (thus giving a specious appearance)
[23] *Which* than which [29] *lunes* fits of lunacy [32] *tongue blister* (because
lies were supposed to blister the tongue) [33-34] *red-looked . . . trumpet*
(the figure is of an angry face as a herald dressed in red and preceded
by a trumpet[er])

That your free undertaking cannot miss
A thriving issue: there is no lady living
So meet° for this great errand. Please your ladyship   45
To visit the next room, I'll presently°
Acquaint the Queen of your most noble offer,
Who but today hammered of° this design,
But durst not tempt° a minister of honor
Lest she should be denied.

Paulina.   Tell her, Emilia,   50
I'll use that tongue I have; if wit° flow from 't
As boldness from my bosom, let 't not be doubted
I shall do good.

Emilia.   Now be you blest for it!
I'll to the Queen. Please you come something nearer.

Jailer. Madam, if 't please the Queen to send the babe,   55
I know not what I shall incur to pass it,°
Having no warrant.

Paulina.   You need not fear it, sir:
This child was prisoner to the womb and is
By law and process of great Nature thence
Freed, and enfranchised; not a party to   60
The anger of the King, nor guilty of,
If any be, the trespass of the Queen.

Jailer. I do believe it.

Paulina. Do not you fear—upon mine honor, I
Will stand betwixt you and danger.   *Exeunt.*   65

---

45 *meet* fitting 46 *presently* immediately 48 *hammered of* deliberated
upon 49 *tempt* make trial of 51 *wit* wisdom 56 *to pass it* (as a result
of allowing it to pass)

Scene III. [*Sicilia, the Court of Leontes.*]

Enter Leontes, Servants, Antigonus, and Lords.

Leontes. Nor night nor day no rest: it is but weakness
    To bear the matter thus, mere weakness. If
    The cause were not in being—part o' th' cause,°
    She, th' adult'ress (for the harlot° king
5   Is quite beyond mine arm, out of the blank
    And level° of my brain, plot-proof); but she,
    I can hook to me—say that she were gone,
    Given to the fire, a moiety° of my rest
    Might come to me again. Who's there?

Servant.   My lord!

Leontes. How does the boy?

10 *First Attendant.* He took good rest tonight; 'tis hoped
    His sickness is discharged.

Leontes.   To see his nobleness!
    Conceiving the dishonor of his mother,
    He straight declined, drooped, took it deeply,
    Fastened, and fixed the shame on 't in himself;
15   Threw off his spirit, his appetite, his sleep,
    And downright languished. Leave me solely; go,
    See how he fares.   [*Exit Servant.*]
                Fie, fie, no thought of him!°
    The very thought of my revenges that way
    Recoil upon me—in himself too mighty,
20   And in his parties, his alliance; let him be,

II.iii.³ *th' cause* (Leontes interrupts himself, remembering that Polixenes is inaccessible, so that only part of the cause of his agony is within his power to destroy)   ⁴ *harlot* lewd   ⁵⁻⁶ *out of the blank/ And level* beyond my range ("blank" is the center of the target; "level" means "aim." The reference is to archery)   ⁸ *moiety* half   ¹⁷ *no thought of him* i.e., of Polixenes

Until a time may serve. For present vengeance
Take it on her. Camillo and Polixenes
Laugh at me, make their pastime at my sorrow;
They should not laugh if I could reach them, nor
Shall she within my power.

> *Enter Paulina [with the Baby].*

Lord.   You must not enter.   25

Paulina. Nay, rather, good my lords, be second to° me.
  Fear you his tyrannous passion more, alas,
  Than the Queen's life? A gracious innocent soul,
  More free° than he is jealous.

Antigonus.   That's enough.

Servant. Madam, he hath not slept tonight, commanded   30
  None should come at him.

Paulina.   Not so hot, good sir;
  I come to bring him sleep. 'Tis such as you
  That creep like shadows by him, and do sigh
  At each his needless heavings—such as you
  Nourish the cause of his awaking. I   35
  Do come with words as medicinal as true,
  Honest as either, to purge him of that humor°
  That presses him from sleep.

Leontes.   What noise there, ho?

Paulina. No noise, my lord, but needful conference
  About some gossips° for your Highness.

Leontes.   How?   40
  Away with that audacious lady! Antigonus,
  I charged thee that she should not come about me;
  I knew she would.

Antigonus.   I told her so, my lord,
  On your displeasure's peril, and on mine,
  She should not visit you.

Leontes.   What? Canst not rule her?   45

---

²⁶ *be second to* support ²⁹ *free* innocent ³⁷ *humor* illness ⁴⁰ *gossips*
godparents

Paulina. From all dishonesty he can: in this,
　　Unless he take the course that you have done—
　　Commit me for committing° honor, trust it,
　　He shall not rule me.

Antigonus.　　　　　　　La you now, you hear,
50　　When she will take the rein, I let her run;
　　But she'll not stumble.°

Paulina.　　　　　　　Good my liege, I come—
　　And I beseech you hear me, who profess
　　Myself your loyal servant, your physician,
　　Your most obedient counselor; yet that dares
55　　Less appear so in comforting° you evils,
　　Than such as most seem yours°—I say, I come
　　From your good queen.

Leontes.　　　　　　　Good queen!

Paulina. Good queen, my lord, good queen, I say good
　　　　queen,
　　And would by combat° make her good, so were I
　　A man, the worst° about you.

60　*Leontes.*　　　　　　　Force her hence.

Paulina. Let him that makes but trifles of his eyes
　　First hand me. On mine own accord I'll off,
　　But first I'll do my errand. The good queen
　　(For she is good) hath brought you forth a daughter;
　　Here 'tis; commends it to your blessing.

　　　　　　　　　　[*She lays down the Baby.*]

65　*Leontes.*　　　　　　　Out!
　　A mankind° witch! Hence with her, out o' door!

---

⁴⁸ *Commit . . . committing* (the word is used in a punning sense, first
meaning "send to prison," and secondly, "performing") ⁵⁰⁻⁵¹ *rein
. . . run . . . stumble* (Antigonus, as usual, speaks of his wife as if
she were a horse) ⁵⁵ *comforting* abetting, countenancing ⁵⁶ *as most
seems yours* as are nearest to you ⁵⁹ *by combat* in a trial by combat
(which would, in the code of chivalry, vindicate a lady's honor)
⁶⁰ *the worst* the lowest in degree ⁶⁶ *mankind* male, ferocious, violent

A most intelligencing° bawd!

Paulina.   Not so;
  I am as ignorant in that as you
  In so entitling me; and no less honest
  Than you are mad; which is enough, I'll warrant,   70
  As this world goes, to pass for honest.

Leontes.   Traitors!
  Will you not push her out? [*To Antigonus*] Give
    her the bastard,
  Thou dotard, thou art woman-tired,° unroosted
  By thy Dame Partlet° here. Take up the bastard,
  Take 't up, I say; give 't to thy crone.

Paulina.   Forever   75
  Unvenerable be thy hands, if thou
  Tak'st up the Princess, by that forcèd baseness°
  Which he has put upon 't!

Leontes.   He dreads his wife.

Paulina. So I would you did; then 'twere past all doubt
  You'd call your children yours.

Leontes.   A nest of traitors.   80

Antigonus. I am none, by this good light.

Paulina.   Nor I: nor any
  But one that's here, and that's himself; for he,
  The sacred honor of himself, his queen's,
  His hopeful son's, his babe's, betrays to slander,
  Whose sting is sharper than the sword's; and will not   85
  (For as the case now stands, it is a curse
  He cannot be compelled to 't) once remove
  The root of his opinion, which is rotten
  As ever oak or stone was sound.

Leontes.   A callat°
  Of boundless tongue, who late hath beat her hus-
    band,   90

---

⁶⁷ *intelligencing* i.e., acting as a pander   ⁷³ *woman-tired* henpecked
⁷⁴ *Dame Partlet* (traditionally the name of the hen; compare Reynard
the fox, etc.)   ⁷⁷ *forcèd baseness* falsely base name (bastard)   ⁸⁹ *callat*
scold

And now baits° me! This brat is none of mine;
It is the issue of Polixenes.
Hence with it, and together with the dam,
Commit them to the fire.

Paulina.   It is yours:
95 And might we lay th' old proverb° to your charge,
So like you, 'tis the worse. Behold, my lords,
Although the print be little, the whole matter
And copy° of the father: eye, nose, lip,
The trick of 's frown, his forehead, nay, the valley,
The pretty dimples of his chin and cheek; his
100   smiles;
The very mold and frame of hand, nail, finger.
And thou, good goddess Nature, which hast made it
So like to him that got° it, if thou hast
The ordering of the mind too, 'mongst all colors
105 No yellow° in 't, lest she suspect, as he does,
Her children not her husband's.

Leontes.   A gross hag!
And lozel,° thou art worthy to be hanged,
That wilt not stay her tongue.

Antigonus.   Hang all the husbands
That cannot do that feat, you'll leave yourself
Hardly one subject.

110 *Leontes.*   Once more, take her hence.

Paulina. A most unworthy and unnatural lord
Can do no more.

Leontes.   I'll ha' thee burned.

Paulina.   I care not;
It is an heretic that makes the fire,
Not she which burns in 't. I'll not call you tyrant;
115 But this most cruel usage of your queen
(Not able to produce more accusation

90–91 *beat . . . baits* (pronounced alike)   95 *th' old proverb* i.e., "They are so like that they are the worse for it"   97–98 *print . . . matter . . . copy* (the figure is derived from printing)   103 *got* begot   105 *yellow* (the color of jealousy)   107 *lozel* worthless fellow

Than your own weak-hinged° fancy) something
  savors
Of tyranny, and will ignoble make you,
Yea, scandalous to the world.

Leontes.   On your allegiance,°
  Out of the chamber with her! Were I a tyrant,°   *120*
  Where were her life? She durst not call me so,
  If she did know me one. Away with her.

Paulina. I pray you do not push me, I'll be gone.
  Look to your babe, my lord, 'tis yours: Jove send her
  A better guiding spirit. What needs these hands?   *125*
  You, that are thus so tender o'er his follies,
  Will never do him good, not one of you.
  So, so; farewell, we are gone.   *Exit.*

Leontes. Thou, traitor, hast set on thy wife to this.
  My child? Away with 't! Even thou, that hast   *130*
  A heart so tender o'er it, take it hence,
  And see it instantly consumed with fire.
  Even thou, and none but thou. Take it up straight;
  Within this hour bring me word 'tis done,
  And by good testimony, or I'll seize° thy life,   *135*
  With what thou else call'st thine; if thou refuse,
  And wilt encounter with my wrath, say so;
  The bastard brains with these my proper° hands
  Shall I dash out. Go, take it to the fire,
  For thou sett'st on thy wife.

Antigonus.   I did not, sir;   *140*
  These lords, my noble fellows, if they please,
  Can clear me in 't.

Lords.   We can: my royal liege,
  He is not guilty of her coming hither.

Leontes. You're liars all.

---

[117] *weak-hinged* ill-supported (a door hangs on its hinges)   [119] *On your allegiance* (the ultimate command; to disobey it is treason)   [120] *tyrant* (Paulina avoided calling him tyrant, but in coming close to so doing reminded him that this interpretation might all too easily be put upon his actions)   [135] *seize* confiscate   [138] *proper* own

145 *Lord.* Beseech your Highness, give us better credit.
    We have always truly served you, and beseech
    So to esteem of us; and on our knees we beg,
    As recompense of our dear services
    Past, and to come, that you do change this purpose,
150 Which being so horrible, so bloody, must
    Lead on to some foul issue. We all kneel.

Leontes. I am a feather for each wind that blows.
    Shall I live on to see this bastard kneel
    And call me father? Better burn it now
155 Than curse it then. But be it; let it live.
    It shall not neither. You, sir, come you hither:
    You that have been so tenderly officious
    With Lady Margery,° your midwife there,
    To save this bastard's life—for 'tis a bastard,
    So sure as this beard's gray° —what will you adven-
160   ture,
    To save this brat's life?

Antigonus.   Anything, my lord,
    That my ability may undergo,
    And nobleness impose—at least thus much:
    I'll pawn° the little blood which I have left,
165 To save the innocent—anything possible.

Leontes. It shall be possible. Swear by this sword°
    Thou wilt perform my bidding.

Antigonus.   I will, my lord.

Leontes. Mark, and perform it: seest thou? For the
    fail°
    Of any point in 't, shall not only be
170 Death to thyself, but to thy lewd-tongued wife,
    Whom for this time we pardon. We enjoin thee,
    As thou art liegeman to us, that thou carry
    This female bastard hence, and that thou bear it
    To some remote and desert place, quite out

---

158 *Lady Margery* (another facetious name of the hen)   160 *this beard's gray* (Leontes here, presumably, refers to—perhaps touches—the beard of Antigonus)   164 *pawn* pledge   166 *by this sword* by the cross on the handle, or that formed by the hilt and the blade   168 *fail* failure

Of our dominions; and that there thou leave it,   *175*
Without more mercy, to its own protection
And favor of the climate. As by strange fortune
It came to us, I do in justice charge thee,
On thy soul's peril, and thy body's torture,
That thou commend it strangely° to some place,   *180*
Where chance may nurse or end it. Take it up.

Antigonus. I swear to do this, though a present death
  Had been more merciful. Come on, poor babe,
  Some powerful spirit instruct the kites and ravens
  To be thy nurses! Wolves and bears, they say,   *185*
  Casting their savageness aside, have done
  Like offices of pity. Sir, be prosperous
  In more than this deed does require!° And blessing
  Against this cruelty fight on thy side,
  Poor thing, condemned to loss. *Exit* [*with the Baby*].

Leontes.   No, I'll not rear   *190*
  Another's issue.

                    Enter a Servant.

Servant.   Please your Highness, posts
  From those you sent to th' oracle are come
  An hour since: Cleomenes and Dion,
  Being well arrived from Delphos, are both landed,
  Hasting to th' court.

Lord.   So please you, sir, their speed   *195*
  Hath been beyond accompt.°

Leontes.   Twenty-three days
  They have been absent; 'tis good speed; foretells
  The great Apollo suddenly will have
  The truth of this appear. Prepare you, lords,
  Summon a session,° that we may arraign   *200*
  Our most disloyal lady; for as she hath
  Been publicly accused, so shall she have
  A just and open trial. While she lives,
  My heart will be a burden to me. Leave me,
  And think upon my bidding.   *Exeunt.* *205*

---

180 *strangely* as a stranger   188 *require* deserve   196 *beyond accompt*
unprecedented   200 *session* judicial trial or investigation

ACT III

Scene I. [*Sicilia. On a high road.*]

Enter Cleomenes and Dion.

Cleomenes. The climate's delicate, the air most sweet,
Fertile the isle,° the temple much surpassing
The common praise it bears.

Dion.   I shall report,
For most it caught me, the celestial habits°
5   (Methinks I so should term them) and the reverence
Of the grave wearers. O, the sacrifice,
How ceremonious, solemn, and unearthly
It was i' th' off'ring!

Cleomenes.   But of all, the burst
And the ear-deaf'ning voice o' th' oracle,
10   Kin to Jove's thunder, so surprised my sense,
That I was nothing.

Dion.   If th' event° o' th' journey
Prove as successful to the Queen (O be 't so!)
As it hath been to us rare, pleasant, speedy,
The time is worth the use on 't.

Cleomenes.   Great Apollo
15   Turn all to th' best; these proclamations,

III.i.² *the isle* i.e., Delos (as in II.i.¹⁸³; again by mistake for Delphi)
⁴ *celestial habits* heavenly clothing   ¹¹ *event* outcome

So forcing faults upon Hermione,
I little like.

Dion.   The violent carriage° of it
Will clear or end the business when the oracle,
Thus by Apollo's great divine° sealed up,
Shall the contents discover, something rare   20
Even then will rush to knowledge. Go; fresh horses,
And gracious be the issue!   *Exeunt.*

Scene II. [*Sicilia, a court of justice.*]

Enter Leontes, Lords, Officers.

Leontes. This session, to our great grief we pronounce,
Even pushes 'gainst our heart. The party tried,
The daughter of a king, our wife, and one
Of us too much beloved. Let us be cleared
Of being tyrannous, since we so openly   5
Proceed in justice, which shall have due course,
Even to the guilt or the purgation.°
Produce the prisoner.

Officer. It is his Highness' pleasure that the Queen
Appear in person here in court.

[*Enter*] *Hermione, as to her trial,*° [*Paulina and*]
Ladies.
                              Silence.°   10

Leontes. Read the indictment.

Officer. "Hermione, Queen to the worthy Leontes, King
of Sicilia, thou art here accused and arraigned of high

---

¹⁷ *carriage* management   ¹⁹ *great divine* chief priest   III.ii.⁷ *purgation*
acquittal   ¹⁰ s.d. *as to her trial* (this direction occurs in the Folio at
the head of the scene)   ¹⁰ *Silence* (italic in Folio, as if a stage direction.
But presumably the Officer calls out the word)

treason, in committing adultery with Polixenes, King
15 of Bohemia, and conspiring with Camillo to take away
the life of our sovereign lord the King, thy royal husband; the pretense° whereof being by circumstances
partly laid open, thou, Hermione, contrary to the faith
and allegiance of a true subject, didst counsel and aid
20 them, for their better safety, to fly away by night."

Hermione. Since what I am to say must be but that
    Which contradicts my accusation, and
    The testimony on my part no other
    But what comes from myself, it shall scarce boot°
      me
25   To say, "Not guilty"; mine integrity
    Being counted falsehood, shall, as I express it,
    Be so received. But thus: if powers divine
    Behold our human actions—as they do—
    I doubt not then, but Innocence shall make
30   False Accusation blush, and Tyranny
    Tremble at Patience. You, my lord, best know—
    Who least will seem to do so—my past life
    Hath been as continent, as chaste, as true,
    As I am now unhappy; which is more
35   Than history can pattern,° though devised
    And played to take° spectators. For behold me,
    A fellow of the royal bed, which owe°
    A moiety of the throne, a great king's daughter,
    The mother to a hopeful prince, here standing
40   To prate and talk for life and honor, 'fore
    Who please to come and hear. For life, I prize it
    As I weigh grief, which I would spare; for honor,
    'Tis a derivative from me to mine,°
    And only that I stand for. I appeal
45   To your own conscience, sir, before Polixenes
    Came to your court, how I was in your grace,
    How merited to be so; since he came,
    With what encounter so uncurrent, I

---

17 *pretense* design 24 *boot* assist 35 *can pattern* can offer parallels
36 *take* move 37 *owe* own 43 *'Tis . . . mine* i.e., it is my son's inheritance

Have strained t' appear thus;° if one jot beyond
The bound of honor, or in act or will   50
That way inclining,° hardened be the hearts
Of all that hear me, and my near'st of kin
Cry fie upon my grave!

Leontes.   I ne'er heard yet
That any of these bolder vices wanted
Less impudence to gainsay what they did,   55
Than to perform it first.°

Hermione.   That's true enough,
Though 'tis a saying, sir, not due to me.

Leontes. You will not own it.

Hermione.   More than mistress of
Which comes to me in name of fault, I must not
At all acknowledge.° For Polixenes,   60
With whom I am accused, I do confess
I loved him, as in honor he required;°
With such a kind of love, as might become
A lady like me; with a love, even such,
So, and no other, as yourself commanded;   65
Which not to have done, I think had been in me
Both disobedience and ingratitude
To you, and toward your friend, whose love had
    spoke,
Even since it could speak, from an infant, freely,
That it was yours. Now, for conspiracy,   70
I know not how it tastes, though it be dished°
For me to try how; all I know of it,
Is that Camillo was an honest man;
And why he left your court, the gods themselves,
Wotting° no more than I, are ignorant.   75

---

⁴⁸⁻⁴⁹ *With what . . . appear thus* by what outrageous conduct I have
acted so unlike myself as to bring upon myself the ordeal of this
appearance in court ⁵⁰⁻⁵¹ *or in act . . . inclining* either in performance or intention approaching the bounds of honor ⁵⁵⁻⁵⁶ *Less
impudence . . . first* (the point is that if one is bold enough to commit the crime one will be bold enough to deny it; but the expression is
not very clear) ⁵⁸⁻⁶⁰ *More than mistress . . . acknowledge* I must
refuse to acknowledge as my own, faults which I do not in fact possess
⁶² *required* was entitled to ⁷¹ *dished* served (as of food) ⁷⁵ *Wotting*
if they know

Leontes. You knew of his departure, as you know
     What you have underta'en to do in 's absence.

Hermione.   Sir,
     You speak a language that I understand not.
     My life stands in the level° of your dreams,
     Which I'll lay down.

80 *Leontes.*   Your actions are my dreams.
     You had a bastard by Polixenes,
     And I but dreamed it. As you were past all shame—
     Those of your fact° are so—so past all truth;
     Which to deny concerns more than avails;° for as
85   Thy brat hath been cast out, like to itself,°
     No father owning it (which is indeed
     More criminal in thee than it) so thou
     Shalt feel our justice; in whose easiest passage
     Look for no less than death.

     Hermione.   Sir, spare your threats:
90   The bug° which you would fright me with, I seek.
     To me can life be no commodity.°
     The crown and comfort of my life, your favor,
     I do give° lost, for I do feel it gone,
     But know not how it went. My second joy,
95   And first fruits of my body, from his presence
     I am barred, like one infectious. My third comfort,
     Starred° most unluckily, is from my breast,
     The innocent milk in its most innocent mouth,
     Haled out to murder. Myself on every post°
100 Proclaimed a strumpet; with immodest hatred
     The childbed privilege denied, which 'longs°
     To women of all fashion.° Lastly, hurried

---

79 *level* range (archery) 83 *Those of your fact* those guilty of your
crime 84 *concerns more than avails* is more trouble to you than it's
worth 85 *like to itself* i.e., appropriately, since it has no father 90 *bug*
bogey, bugbear 91 *commodity* advantage, asset 93 *give* reckon as
97 *starred* fated 99 *post* (on which public notices and advertisements
were placed. In Greene's novel the King issues a proclamation concerning his wife's guilt, which is "blazed through the country") 101 *longs*
belongs 102 *fashion* rank

Here to this place, i' th' open air, before
I have got strength of limit.° Now, my liege,
Tell me, what blessings I have here alive,   105
That I should fear to die? Therefore proceed.
But yet hear this—mistake me not: for life,
I prize it not a straw, but for mine honor,
Which I would free—if I shall be condemned
Upon surmises, all proofs sleeping else   110
But what your jealousies awake, I tell you
'Tis rigor, and not law.° Your honors all,
I do refer me to the oracle:
Apollo be my judge!

Lord.   This your request
Is altogether just; therefore bring forth,   115
And in Apollo's name, his oracle. [*Exeunt Officers.*]

Hermione. The Emperor of Russia° was my father.
Oh that he were alive, and here beholding
His daughter's trial! That he did but see
The flatness° of my misery; yet with eyes   120
Of pity, not revenge!

    [*Enter Officers, with*] Cleomenes [*and*] Dion.

Officer. You here shall swear upon this sword of
    justice,
That you, Cleomenes and Dion, have
Been both at Delphos, and from thence have brought
This sealed-up oracle, by the hand delivered   125
Of great Apollo's priest; and that since then
You have not dared to break the holy seal,
Nor read the secrets in 't.

Cleomenes, Dion.   All this we swear.

Leontes. Break up the seals and read.

Officer. "Hermione is chaste, Polixenes blameless, Ca-   130
millo a true subject, Leontes a jealous tyrant, his
innocent babe truly begotten, and the King shall live
without an heir, if that which is lost be not found."

---

¹⁰⁴ *strength of limit* strength to go out ¹¹² *rigor, and not law* tyranny,
not justice ¹¹⁷ *Emperor of Russia* (in *Pandosto* it is the wife of
Polixenes who is daughter of this emperor) ¹²⁰ *flatness* completeness

Lords. Now blessèd be the great Apollo!

Hermione.   Praised!

Leontes. Hast thou read truth?

135 *Officer.*   Ay, my lord, even so
As it is here set down.

Leontes. There is no truth at all i' th' oracle.
The sessions shall proceed; this is mere falsehood.

[*Enter a Servant.*]

Servant. My lord, the King, the King!

Leontes.   What is the business?

140 *Servant.* O sir, I shall be hated to report it.
The Prince, your son, with mere conceit° and fear
Of the Queen's speed,° is gone.

Leontes.   How? Gone?

Servant.   Is dead.

Leontes. Apollo's angry, and the heavens themselves
Do strike at my injustice. [*Hermione faints.*] How
now there!

Paulina. This news is mortal° to the Queen—look
145 down
And see what death is doing.

Leontes.   Take her hence;
Her heart is but o'ercharged, she will recover.
I have too much believed mine own suspicion.
Beseech you tenderly apply to her
Some remedies for life.

[*Exeunt Paulina and Ladies, with Hermione.*]

150   Apollo, pardon
My great profaneness 'gainst thine oracle.
I'll reconcile me to Polixenes,
New woo my queen, recall the good Camillo—

---

141 *conceit* concept, thought   142 *speed* fortune, success   145 *mortal*
deadly

Whom I proclaim a man of truth, of mercy.
For, being transported by my jealousies   155
To bloody thoughts and to revenge, I chose
Camillo for the minister to poison
My friend Polixenes; which had been done,
But that the good mind of Camillo tardied
My swift command, though I with death and with   160
Reward did threaten and encourage him,
Not doing it and being done.° He, most humane,
And filled with honor, to my kingly guest
Unclasped my practice,° quit his fortunes here—
Which you knew great—and to the hazard°   165
Of all incertainties himself commended,
No richer than his honor. How he glisters
Through my rust!° And how his piety
Does my deeds make the blacker!

[*Enter Paulina.*]

Paulina.   Woe the while!
O cut my lace,° lest my heart, cracking it,   170
Break too!

Lord. What fit is this, good lady?

Paulina. What studied torments, tyrant, hast for me?
What wheels, racks, fires? What flaying, boiling
In leads or oils? What old or newer torture   175
Must I receive, whose every word deserves
To taste of thy most worst. Thy tyranny,
Together working with thy jealousies,
Fancies too weak for boys, too green and idle
For girls of nine—O, think what they have done,   180
And then run mad indeed, stark mad; for all

160-62 *though I . . . being done* though I threatened him with death
for not doing it, and promised him rewards for doing it   164 *Unclasped my practice* revealed my plot   165 *Which . . . hazard* (the line
apparently lacks a foot, which the Second Folio—with the approval of
some editors—supplies by inserting the word "certain" before "hazard")
168 *Through my rust* (again, to mend the meter, F2 reads "through my
dark rust." Some editors read "Thorough," which is interchangeable with
"Through")   170 *cut my lace* (to give her more breath)

Thy bygone fooleries were but spices° of it.
That thou betrayedst Polixenes, 'twas nothing;
That did but show thee, of a fool,° inconstant,
185 And damnable ingrateful. Nor was 't much
Thou wouldst have poisoned good Camillo's honor,
To have him kill a king—poor trespasses,
More monstrous standing by;° whereof I reckon
The casting forth to crows thy baby daughter
190 To be or none, or little; though a devil
Would have shed water out of fire,° ere done 't;
Nor is t' directly laid to thee the death
Of the young Prince, whose honorable thoughts,
Thoughts high for one so tender, cleft the heart
195 That could conceive a gross and foolish sire
Blemished his gracious dam. This is not, no,
Laid to thy answer; but the last—O lords,
When I have said,° cry "woe": the Queen, the
        Queen,
The sweet'st, dear'st creature's dead; and vengeance
        for 't
Not dropped down yet.

200 *Lords.*   The higher pow'rs forbid!

Paulina. I say she's dead; I'll swear 't. If word nor oath
Prevail not, go and see; if you can bring
Tincture or luster in her lip, her eye,
Heat outwardly or breath within, I'll serve you
205 As I would do the gods. But, O thou tyrant,
Do not repent these things, for they are heavier
Than all thy woes can stir;° therefore betake thee
To nothing but despair. A thousand knees,
Ten thousand years together, naked, fasting,
210 Upon a barren mountain, and still winter°
In storm perpetual, could not move the gods
To look that way thou wert.

Leontes.   Go on, go on;

---

182 *spices* samples 184 *of a fool* for a fool 188 *standing by* i.e., and so
available for comparison 191 *shed water out of fire* wept out of burning eyes 198 *said* said it 207 *all thy woes can stir* all thy penitence can
remove 218 *still winter* forever winter

Thou canst not speak too much, I have deserved
All tongues to talk their bitt'rest.

Lord.   Say no more;
Howe'er the business goes, you have made fault   215
I' th' boldness of your speech.

Paulina.   I am sorry for 't;
All faults I make, when I shall come to know them,
I do repent. Alas, I have showed too much
The rashness of a woman; he is touched
To th' noble heart. What's gone and what's past
    help   220
Should be past grief; do not receive affliction
At my petition;° I beseech you, rather
Let me be punished that have minded you
Of what you should forget. Now, good my liege,
Sir, royal sir, forgive a foolish woman.   225
The love I bore your queen—lo, fool again!
I'll speak of her no more, nor of your children;
I'll not remember° you of my own lord,
Who is lost too. Take your patience to you,
And I'll say nothing.

Leontes.   Thou didst speak but well,   230
When most the truth° which I receive much better
Than to be pitied of thee. Prithee bring me
To the dead bodies of my queen and son.
One grave shall be for both; upon them shall
The causes of their death appear, unto   235
Our shame perpetual. Once a day I'll visit
The chapel where they lie, and tears shed there
Shall be my recreation.° So long as nature
Will bear up with this exercise, so long
I daily vow to use it. Come, and lead me   240
To these sorrows.   *Exeunt.*

---

²²¹⁻²² *do not receive . . . petition* I would not have you suffer because
I prayed that you should   ²²⁸ *remember* remind   ²³⁰⁻³¹ *Thou didst
. . . the truth* You spoke well only when most telling the truth   ²³⁸ *recreation* diversion (to do so will be his only pastime)

Scene III. [*Bohemia,*° *the seacoast.*]

Enter Antigonus [*and*] *a Mariner,* [*with a*] *Babe.*

Antigonus. Thou art perfect° then our ship hath
     touched upon
The deserts of Bohemia?

Mariner.   Ay, my lord, and fear
We have landed in ill time; the skies look grimly,
And threaten present blusters. In my conscience, °
5 The heavens with that we have in hand are angry
And frown upon 's.

Antigonus. Their sacred wills be done! Go get aboard,
Look to thy bark, I'll not be long before
I call upon thee.

Mariner.   Make your best haste, and go not
10 Too far i' th' land; 'tis like to be loud weather;
Besides, this place is famous for the creatures
Of prey that keep° upon 't.

Antigonus.   Go thou away,
I'll follow instantly.

Mariner.   I am glad at heart
To be so rid o' th' business.   *Exit.*

Antigonus.   Come, poor babe;
15 I have heard, but not believed, the spirits o' th' dead
May walk again; if such thing be,° thy mother
Appeared to me last night; for ne'er was dream

III.iii.s.d. *Bohemia* (substituted for the Sicily of *Pandosto.* Bohemia, as
is notorious, had no seacoast)   [1] *perfect* certain   [4] *conscience* knowledge, awareness (but with something of the modern meaning also)
[12] *keep* live   [16] *if such thing be* (Antigonus takes the skeptical Protestant
view as a rule, but is convinced of the reality of the vision. Possibly
Shakespeare, when he wrote this scene, had not yet had the idea of
reanimating Hermione)

So like awaking. To me comes a creature,
Sometimes her head on one side, some another;
I never saw a vessel of like sorrow   20
So filled, and so becoming.° In pure white robes,
Like very sanctity,° she did approach
My cabin° where I lay; thrice bowed before me,
And, gasping to begin some speech, her eyes
Became two spouts; the fury spent, anon   25
Did this break from her: "Good Antigonus,
Since fate, against thy better disposition,
Hath made thy person for the thrower-out
Of my poor babe, according to thine oath,
Places remote enough are in Bohemia,   30
There weep, and leave it crying; and for the babe
Is counted lost forever, Perdita°
I prithee call 't. For this ungentle business
Put on thee by my lord, thou ne'er shalt see
Thy wife Paulina more." And so, with shrieks,   35
She melted into air. Affrighted much,
I did in time collect myself, and thought
This was so,° and no slumber. Dreams are toys;°
Yet for this once, yea superstitiously,°
I will be squared° by this. I do believe   40
Hermione hath suffered death, and that
Apollo would (this being indeed the issue
Of King Polixenes) it should here be laid
Either for life, or death, upon the earth
Of its right father. Blossom, speed thee well!   45

[*He lays down the Baby.*]

There lie, and there thy character:° there these,

[*Lays down a bundle.*]

Which may, if Fortune please, both breed thee,°
    pretty,

---

²¹ *so filled and so becoming* so filled with sorrow, and so beautiful in
sorrow   ²² *very sanctity* sanctity itself   ²³ *cabin* berth   ³² *Perdita*
(meaning "the lost girl")   ³⁸ *This was so* this was real   ³⁸ *toys* trifles
³⁹ *superstitiously* (again the Protestant view of ghosts)   ⁴⁰ *squared*
regulated, ordered   ⁴⁶ *character* description (by which Perdita is later
to be recognized)   ⁴⁷ *breed thee* raise you, pay for your upbringing

And still rest thine.° The storm begins; poor wretch,
That for thy mother's fault art thus exposed
50   To loss, and what may follow! Weep I cannot,°
But my heart bleeds; and most accursed am I
To be by oath enjoined to this. Farewell,
The day frowns more and more; thou 'rt like to have
A lullaby too rough; I never saw
55   The heavens so dim by day. A savage clamor!°
Well may I get aboard! This is the chase;°
I am gone forever.   *Exit, pursued by a bear.*

[*Enter*] *Shepherd.*

Shepherd. I would there were no age between ten and
three-and-twenty, or that youth would sleep out the
60   rest; for there is nothing in the between but getting
wenches with child, wronging the ancientry, stealing,
fighting. Hark you now! Would any but these
boiled° brains of nineteen and two-and-twenty hunt
this weather? They have scared away two of my
65   best sheep, which I fear the wolf will sooner find
than the master; if anywhere I have them, 'tis by
the seaside, browsing of ivy.° Good luck, an 't be
thy will, what have we here? Mercy on 's, a barne!°
A very pretty barne; a boy or a child,° I wonder?
70   A pretty one, a very pretty one; sure, some scape;°
though I am not bookish, yet I can read waiting-
gentlewoman in the scape. This has been some stair-
work, some trunk-work,° some behind-door-work;
they were warmer that got this than the poor thing
75   is here. I'll take it up for pity; yet I'll tarry till my
son come; he hallowed but even now. Whoa-ho-
hoa!

---

⁴⁸ *And still rest thine* there will be something over   ⁵⁰ *Weep I cannot* (though the ghost had told him to)   ⁵⁵ *savage clamor* the noise
of the hunters   ⁵⁶ *chase* the bear   ⁶³ *boiled* seething, hot   ⁶⁷ *browsing of ivy* ("whereon they do greatly feed," according to *Pandosto*)
⁶⁸ *barne* child (compare mod. Scots "bairn")   ⁶⁹ *a boy or a child* a boy
or a girl ("child" for "girl" is a dialect form and presumably was so in
1610)   ⁷⁰ *scape* sexual misadventure   ⁷³ *trunk-work* secret or clandes-
tine action

Enter Clown.

Clown. Hilloa, loa!

Shepherd. What? Art so near? If thou 'lt see a thing to
talk on, when thou art dead and rotten, come hither. 80
What ail'st thou, man?

Clown. I have seen two such sights, by sea and by land!
But I am not to say it is a sea, for it is now the sky;
betwixt the firmament and it, you cannot thrust a
bodkin's point. 85

Shepherd. Why, boy, how is it?

Clown. I would you did but see how it chafes, how
it rages, how it takes up° the shore, but that's not
to the point. O, the most piteous cry of the poor
souls! Sometimes to see 'em, and not to see 'em; 90
now the ship boring the moon with her mainmast,
and anon swallowed with yeast and froth, as you'd
thrust a cork into a hogshead. And then for the
land-service,° to see how the bear tore out his
shoulder bone, how he cried to me for help, and 95
said his name was Antigonus, a nobleman! But to
make an end of the ship, to see how the sea flap-
dragoned° it; but first, how the poor souls roared,
and the sea mocked them; and how the poor
gentleman roared, and the bear mocked him, both 100
roaring louder than the sea or weather.

Shepherd. Name of mercy, when was this, boy?

Clown. Now, now; I have not winked since I saw these
sights; the men are not yet cold under water, nor
the bear half dined on the gentleman; he's at it now. 105

Shepherd. Would I had been by, to have helped the
old man!

Clown. I would you had been by the ship's side, to have

---

88 *takes up* rebukes **94** *land-service* i.e., the soldier who serves on
land (Antigonus) as opposed to the seamen aboard the ship (perhaps with a pun on "service" meaning "dish"—Antigonus being food
for the bear) **97-98** *flapdragoned* swallowed down (as drinkers swallowed flapdragons [raisins, etc.] out of burning brandy)

helped her; there your charity would have lacked
110 footing.°

Shepherd. Heavy matters, heavy matters! But look
thee here, boy. Now bless thyself; thou met'st with
things dying, I with things new born. Here's a sight
for thee; look thee, a bearing-cloth° for a squire's
115 child; look thee here, take up, take up, boy; open
it; so, let's see; it was told me I should be rich by
the fairies. This is some changeling;° open 't; what's
within, boy?

Clown. You're a made° old man; if the sins of your
120 youth are forgiven you, you're well to live. Gold,
all gold!

Shepherd. This is fairy gold, boy, and 'twill prove so;
up with 't, keep it close;° home, home, the next°
way! We are lucky, boy, and to be so still° requires
125 nothing but secrecy. Let my sheep go; come, good
boy, the next way home.

Clown. Go you the next way with your findings, I'll go
see if the bear be gone from the gentleman, and
how much he hath eaten. They are never curst° but
130 when they are hungry. If there be any of him left,
I'll bury it.

Shepherd. That's a good deed. If thou mayest discern
by that which is left of him what he is, fetch me to
th' sight of him.

135 *Clown.* Marry° will I; and you shall help to put him
i' th' ground.

Shepherd. 'Tis a lucky day, boy, and we'll do good
deeds on 't.

Exeunt.

109-10 *charity . . . footing* (alluding to the establishment of charitable
foundations)   114 *bearing-cloth* christening robe   117 *changeling* (usually the inferior child left by the fairies; here the child they stole, found
with their gold, which must be kept secret)   119 *made* (Folio reads
"mad," but this emendation of Theobald is supported by the parallel
passage in *Pandosto*)   123 *close* secret   123 *next* nearest   124 *still* always
129 *curst* vicious   135 *Marry* indeed (from "By Mary")

ACT IV

Scene I.

Enter Time, the Chorus.

Time. I that please some, try° all, both joy and terror
    Of good and bad; that makes and unfolds error,
    Now take upon me, in the name of Time,
    To use my wings. Impute it not a crime
    To me, or my swift passage, that I slide   5
    O'er sixteen years, and leave the growth untried°
    Of that wide gap, since it is in my pow'r
    To o'erthrow law, and in one self-born hour
    To plant, and o'erwhelm custom.° Let me pass;°
    The same I am, ere ancient'st order was   10
    Or what is now received. I witness to
    The times that brought them in; so shall I do
    To th' freshest things now reigning, and make stale
    The glistering of this present, as my tale
    Now seems to it.° Your patience this allowing,   15
    I turn my glass, and give my scene such growing

IV. i.¹ *try* test   ⁶ *growth untried* (Time asks to be excused from detailed accounts of the interim period and its developments, for instance Perdita's childhood)   ⁸⁻⁹ *law . . . custom* (note the distinction: Time "plants" Custom but not Law. Custom lacks the authority of Law, and relates to erroneous Opinion; hence the contemporary use of the word in attacks on such ceremonies of the Roman Church as seemed to Protestants without Scriptural authority)   ⁹ *Let me pass . . .* (not clear in detail, but the sense is: Let me pass over that gap; I alone remain unchanged from the beginning—and have passed over that far greater gap)   ¹⁴⁻¹⁵ *as my tale . . . to it* as my tale seems stale compared with the play it interrupts

As you had slept between. Leontes leaving—
Th' effects of his fond° jealousies so grieving,
That he shuts up himself—imagine me,
20 Gentle spectators, that I now may be
In fair Bohemia; and remember well,
I mentioned° a son o' th' King's, which Florizel
I now name to you; and with speed so pace
To speak of Perdita, now grown in grace
25 Equal with wond'ring.° What of her ensues
I list not° prophesy; but let Time's news
Be known when 'tis brought forth. A shepherd's
    daughter,
And what to her adheres,° which follows after,°
Is th' argument° of Time. Of this allow,
30 If ever you have spent time worse, ere now;
If never, yet that Time himself doth say,
He wishes earnestly you never may.   *Exit.*

Scene II. [*Bohemia, the Court of Polixenes.*]

Enter Polixenes and Camillo.

Polixenes. I pray thee, good Camillo, be no more
importunate. 'Tis a sickness denying thee anything,
a death to grant this.

Camillo. It is fifteen years since I saw my country;
5 though I have, for the most part, been aired
abroad, I desire to lay my bones there. Besides,
the penitent King, my master, hath sent for me, to
whose feeling sorrows I might be some allay, or I

---

18 *fond* foolish 22 *mentioned* (unless the whole play is thought of as
Time's report, this is not so; various emendations have been suggested,
of which the best is "A mentioned son . . .") 25 *Equal with wond'ring*
to a degree demanding admiration 26 *I list not* I do not care to
28 *adheres* belongs 28 *after* (at this period an acceptable rhyme for
"daughter") 29 *argument* story

o'erween to° think so, which is another spur to my
departure.   10

Polixenes. As thou lov'st me, Camillo, wipe not out the
rest of thy services by leaving me now. The need I
have of thee, thine own goodness hath made. Better
not to have had thee, than thus to want° thee; thou,
having made me businesses, which none, without   15
thee, can sufficiently manage, must either stay to
execute them thyself, or take away with thee the
very services thou hast done; which if I have not
enough considered—as too much I cannot—to be
more thankful to thee shall be my study, and my   20
profit therein the heaping friendships.° Of that fatal
country Sicilia, prithee speak no more, whose very
naming punishes me with the remembrance of that
penitent (as thou call'st him) and reconciled king,
my brother, whose loss of his most precious queen   25
and children are even now to be afresh lamented.
Say to me, when saw'st thou the Prince Florizel, my
son? Kings are no less unhappy, their issue not
being gracious, than they are in losing them when
they have approved their virtues.°   30

Camillo. Sir, it is three days since I saw the Prince.
What his happier affairs may be are to me unknown;
but I have missingly° noted, he is of late much
retired from court, and is less frequent to his
princely exercises° than formerly he hath appeared.   35

Polixenes. I have considered so much, Camillo, and
with some care, so far that I have eyes under my
service, which look upon his removedness;° from
whom I have this intelligence,° that he is seldom
from the house of a most homely shepherd—a man,   40
they say, that from very nothing, and beyond the

IV.ii.⁹ *o'erween* am boastful enough to   ¹⁴ *want* be without   ²¹ *friendships* friendly offices   ²⁸⁻³⁰ *Kings . . . virtues* it is as hard for kings to
bear the disobedience and ill conduct of their children as to lose them
when convinced of their virtues   ³³ *missingly* (because he noted not the
Prince but his absence)   ³⁵ *exercises* military and sporting activities
³⁷⁻³⁸ *so far that . . : removedness* to the extent that I'm having him
watched in the place where he is hiding himself   ³⁹ *intelligence* report

imagination of his neighbors, is grown into an unspeakable estate.

Camillo. I have heard, sir, of such a man, who hath
45   a daughter of most rare note; the report of her is
extended more than can be thought to begin from
such a cottage.

Polixenes. That's likewise part of my intelligence; but,
I fear, the angle° that plucks our son thither. Thou
50   shalt accompany us to the place, where we will, not
appearing what we are, have some question° with
the shepherd; from whose simplicity I think it not
uneasy to get the cause of my son's resort thither.
Prithee be my present partner in this business, and
55   lay aside the thoughts of Sicilia.

Camillo. I willingly obey your command.

Polixenes. My best Camillo! We must disguise ourselves.

                    Exit [Polixenes with Camillo].

Scene III. [*A road near the Shepherd's cottage.*]

Enter Autolycus, singing.

When daffodils begin to peer,
  With heigh the doxy° over the dale,
Why, then comes in the sweet o' the year,
  For the red blood reigns in the winter's pale.°

5   The white sheet bleaching on the hedge,
  With heigh the sweet birds, O how they sing!

49 *angle* fishhook   51 *question* talk   IV.iii.² *doxy* beggar's mistress
4 *pale* (1) enclosure (2) paleness

Doth set my pugging° tooth an edge,
For a quart of ale is a dish for a king.

The lark, that tirra-lirra chants,
    With heigh, with heigh, the thrush and the jay!   10
Are summer songs for me and my aunts°
    While we lie tumbling in the hay.

I have served Prince Florizel, and in my time wore
three-pile,° but now I am out of service.

But shall I go mourn for that, my dear?   15
    The pale moon shines by night;
And when I wander here and there
    I then do most go right.
If tinkers may have leave to live,
    And bear the sow-skin budget,°   20
Then my account I well may give,
    And in the stocks avouch° it.

My traffic is sheets; when the kite builds, look to
lesser linen.° My father named me Autolycus,° who
being, as I am, littered under Mercury,° was like-   25
wise a snapper-up of unconsidered trifles. With die
and drab,° I purchased this caparison, and my
revenue is the silly cheat.° Gallows and knock°
are too powerful on the highway. Beating and hanging are terrors to me; for the life to come, I sleep   30
out the thought of it. A prize, a prize.

---

⁷ *pugging* thieving (to "pug" means to "pull off"; perhaps Autolycus is
thinking of his sheet-stealing; he is all set to begin snatching them off the
hedges)   ¹¹ *aunts* whores   ¹⁴ *three-pile* the best velvet   ²⁰ *sow-skin
budget* pigskin toolbag   ²² *avouch* corroborate   ²³⁻²⁴ *when the kite . . .
linen* (this is a warning. The kite will use bits of household linen for its
nest; Autolycus will snatch your sheets)   ²⁴ *Autolycus* (son of Chione
by Mercury, grandfather of Ulysses; Homer says he excelled in thieving,
and Ovid that "in theft and filching" he "had no peers")   ²⁵ *under
Mercury* under the influence of the star Mercury (Mercury was the
patron of thieves)   ²⁶⁻²⁷ *die and drab* (dice and whores are responsible
for my having no clothes but these)   ²⁸ *silly cheat* simple (petty) theft
²⁸ *knock* beating (the risks of highway robbery, death, or combat on
the road seem too great)

Enter Clown.

Clown. Let me see, every 'leven wether tods,° every
tod yields pound and odd shilling; fifteen hundred
shorn, what comes the wool to?

35 **Autolycus.** [*Aside*] If the springe° hold, the cock's°
mine.

Clown. I cannot do 't without counters. Let me see,
what am I to buy for our sheep-shearing feast?
Three pound of sugar, five pound of currants, rice—
40 what will this sister of mine do with rice? But my
father hath made her mistress of the feast, and she
lays it on. She hath made me four-and-twenty nose-
gays for the shearers (three-man song-men° all, and
very good ones), but they are most of them means°
45 and basses; but one Puritan amongst them, and he
sings psalms to hornpipes.° I must have saffron to
color the warden pies;° mace;° dates, none, that's
out of my note; nutmegs, seven; a race or two of
ginger, but that I may beg; four pound of prunes,
50 and as many of raisins o' th' sun.°

Autolycus. Oh, that ever I was born!

Clown. I' th' name of me!

Autolycus. Oh help me, help me; pluck but off these
rags; and then, death, death!

55 **Clown.** Alack, poor soul, thou hast need of more rags
to lay on thee, rather than have these off.

Autolycus. Oh sir, the loathsomeness of them offends
me more than the stripes I have received, which are
mighty ones and millions.

60 **Clown.** Alas, poor man, a million of beating may come
to a great matter.

---

[32] *every 'leven wether tods* every eleven sheep yield a tod (28 lbs.) of
wool [35] *springe* snare [35] *cock's* woodcock's [43] *three-man song-men*
singers of lively catches for three voices [44] *means* tenors [46] *psalms to
hornpipes* i.e., he is an unusually cheerful Puritan [47] *warden pies* pies
made of warden pears [47] *mace* spice made of nutmeg [50] *o' th' sun*
sun-dried

Autolycus. I am robbed, sir, and beaten; my money and apparel ta'en from me, and these detestable things put upon me.

Clown. What, by a horseman or a footman?°   65

Autolycus. A footman, sweet sir, a footman.

Clown. Indeed, he should be a footman, by the garments he has left with thee; if this be a horseman's coat, it hath seen very hot service. Lend me thy hand, I'll help thee. Come, lend me thy hand.   70

[*Helps him up.*]

Autolycus. Oh good sir, tenderly, oh!

Clown. Alas, poor soul!

Autolycus. Oh good sir, softly, good sir; I fear, sir, my shoulder blade is out.

Clown. How now? Canst stand?   75

Autolycus. Softly, dear sir; good sir, softly; you ha' done me a charitable office.

[*Picks his pocket.*]

Clown. Dost lack any money? I have a little money for thee.

Autolycus. No, good sweet sir; no, I beseech you, sir;   80
I have a kinsman not past three-quarters of a mile hence, unto whom I was going. I shall there have money, or anything I want; offer me no money, I pray you; that kills my heart.

Clown. What manner of fellow was he that robbed   85
you?

Autolycus. A fellow, sir, that I have known to go about with troll-my-dames;° I knew him once a servant of the Prince. I cannot tell, good sir, for which of his virtues it was, but he was certainly whipped out   90
of the court.

Clown. His vices,° you would say; there's no virtue

---

⁶⁵ *footman* foot soldier   ⁸⁸ *troll-my-dames* a game played by women, rather like bagatelle   ⁹² *vices* (the Clown fails to see Autolycus' little joke)

whipped out of the court; they cherish it to make it
stay there; and yet it will no more but abide.°

95 *Autolycus.* Vices, I would say, sir. I know this man
well; he hath been since an ape-bearer;° then a
process-server,° a bailiff: then he compassed a mo-
tion° of the Prodigal Son,° and married a tinker's
wife within a mile where my land and living° lies;
100 and, having flown over many knavish professions,
he settled only in rogue. Some call him Autolycus.

Clown. Out upon him! Prig,° for my life, prig! He
haunts wakes, fairs, and bear-baitings.

105 *Autolycus.* Very true, sir; he, sir, he; that's the rogue
that put me into this apparel.

Clown. Not a more cowardly rogue in all Bohemia; if
you had but looked big, and spit at him, he'd have
run.

110 *Autolycus.* I must confess to you, sir, I am no fighter;
I am false of heart that way, and that he knew, I
warrant him.

Clown. How do you now?

Autolycus. Sweet sir, much better than I was. I can
115 stand and walk. I will even take my leave of you,
and pace softly towards my kinsman's.

Clown. Shall I bring thee on the way?

Autolycus. No, good-faced sir, no, sweet sir.

Clown. Then fare thee well; I must go buy spices for
120 our sheep-shearing.   *Exit.*

Autolycus. Prosper you, sweet sir! Your purse is not
hot enough to purchase your spice. I'll be with you
at your sheep-shearing too; if I make not this cheat

---

⁹⁴ *abide* make a brief stay   ⁹⁶ *ape-bearer* one who carries a monkey
about for exhibition   ⁹⁷ *process-server* server of writs, bailiff   ⁹⁷⁻⁹⁸ *compassed a motion* got possession of a puppet show   ⁹⁸ *Prodigal Son*
(a favorite theme for representation)   ⁹⁹ *land and living* (Autolycus
refers grandly to his estates)   ¹⁰³ *Prig* thief

bring out another, and the shearers prove sheep, let
me be unrolled,° and my name put in the book of   125
virtue!

Song.

Jog on, jog on, the footpath way,
And merrily hent° the stile-a;
A merry heart goes all the day,
Your sad tires in a mile-a.   130

Exit.

Scene IV. [*Bohemia, the Shepherd's cottage.*]

Enter Florizel [and] Perdita.

Florizel. These your unusual weeds° to each part of
   you
   Do give a life; no shepherdess, but Flora,°
   Peering in April's front.° This your sheep-shearing
   Is as a meeting of the petty gods,
   And you the Queen on 't.

Perdita.   Sir, my gracious lord,   5
   To chide at your extremes° it not becomes me—
   Oh pardon, that I name them! Your high self,
   The gracious mark° o' th' land, you have obscured
   With a swain's wearing; and me, poor lowly maid,
   Most goddesslike pranked up. But that our feasts   10
   In every mess have folly, and the feeders
   Digest it with a custom,° I should blush

---

¹²⁵ *unrolled* struck off the honorable list of vagabonds   ¹²⁸ *hent* take
hold of (to leap over)   IV.iv.¹ *unusual weeds* unaccustomed garments
(Perdita is dressed to be mistress of the feast)   ² *Flora* (Perdita's costume may have resembled that of the Roman goddess)   ³ *Peering in
April's front* i.e., Flora in April, when the flowers peep out rather than
boldly appear   ⁶ *extremes* exaggerations   ⁸ *mark* the object of every-
one's attention   ¹⁰⁻¹² *our feasts . . . custom* our feasts, at every social
level, admit licensed folly, which the guests tolerate, calling it a custom

To see you so attired; swoon, I think,
To show myself a glass.

Florizel.   I bless the time
15 When my good falcon made her flight across
Thy father's ground.

Perdita.   Now Jove afford you cause!
To me the difference° forges dread; your greatness
Hath not been used to fear. Even now I tremble
To think your father by some accident
20 Should pass this way, as you did: oh, the fates!
How would he look to see his work, so noble,
Vilely bound up?° What would he say? Or how
Should I, in these my borrowed flaunts,° behold
The sternness of his presence?

Florizel.   Apprehend
25 Nothing but jollity. The gods themselves,
Humbling their deities to love, have taken
The shapes of beasts upon them. Jupiter
Became a bull, and bellowed; the green Neptune
A ram, and bleated; and the fire-robed god,
30 Golden Apollo, a poor humble swain,°
As I seem now. Their transformations
Were never for a piece° of beauty rarer,
Nor in a way° so chaste, since my desires
Run not before mine honor, nor my lusts
Burn hotter than my faith.

35 *Perdita.*   Oh, but sir,
Your resolution cannot hold when 'tis
Opposed, as it must be, by th' power of the King.
One of these two must be necessities,
Which then will speak, that you must change this
    purpose,
Or I my life.°

¹⁷ *difference* i.e., in our ranks   ²² *Vilely bound up* (the analogy is with
a good book shabbily bound)   ²³ *flaunts* finery   ²⁷⁻³⁰ *Jupiter . . .
swain* (Jupiter took the shape of a bull to carry off Europa; Neptune
became a ram to woo Theophane; Apollo served as a shepherd to help
Admetus win Alcestis)   ³² *piece* work of art   ³³ *in a way* (he refers
to the chastity of his intentions, not to Perdita herself)   ³⁸⁻⁴⁰ *One of
these two . . . I my life* i.e., the time will come when Florizel will have
to give up his plans, or Perdita will lose her life

Florizel.   Thou dearest Perdita,   40
  With these forced° thoughts, I prithee, darken not
  The mirth o' th' feast: or I'll be thine, my fair,
  Or° not my father's. For I cannot be
  Mine own, nor anything to any, if
  I be not thine. To this I am most constant,   45
  Though destiny say no. Be merry, gentle;
  Strangle such thoughts as these, with anything
  That you behold the while. Your guests are coming;
  Lift up your countenance, as it were the day
  Of celebration of that nuptial, which   50
  We two have sworn shall come.

Perdita.   O Lady Fortune,
  Stand you auspicious!

Florizel.   See, your guests approach.
  Address yourself to entertain them sprightly,
  And let's be red with mirth.

    [Enter] Shepherd, Clown, Polixenes, Camillo
    [disguised], Mopsa, Dorcas, Servants.

Shepherd. Fie, daughter! When my old wife lived, upon   55
  This day, she was both pantler,° butler, cook;
  Both dame and servant; welcomed all, served all;
  Would sing her song, and dance her turn; now here
  At upper end o' th' table, now i' th' middle;
  On his shoulder,° and his; her face o' fire   60
  With labor and the thing she took to quench it,
  She would to each one sip. You are retired,°
  As if you were a feasted one, and not
  The hostess of the meeting. Pray you bid
  These unknown friends to 's welcome, for it is   65
  A way to make us better friends, more known.
  Come, quench your blushes, and present yourself
  That which you are, mistress o' th' feast. Come on,
  And bid us welcome to your sheep-shearing,
  As your good flock shall prosper.

Perdita.   *[To Polixenes]* Sir,
  welcome.   70

---

⁴¹ *forced* strained, unduly fearful   ⁴²⁻⁴³ *or . . . Or* either . . . or
⁵⁶ *pantler* keeper of the pantry   ⁶⁰ *on his shoulder* at his shoulder
⁶² *retired* withdrawn

It is my father's will I should take on me
The hostess-ship o' th' day. [*To Camillo*] You're
   welcome, sir.
Give me those flow'rs there, Dorcas. Reverend sirs,
For you there's rosemary and rue; these keep
75 Seeming and savor° all the winter long.
Grace and remembrance° be to you both,
And welcome to our shearing!

Polixenes.   Shepherdess—
A fair one are you—well you fit our ages
With flow'rs of winter.

Perdita.   Sir, the year growing ancient,
80 Not yet on summer's death, nor on the birth
Of trembling winter, the fairest flow'rs o' th' season
Are our carnations, and streaked gillyvors,°
Which some call Nature's bastards;° of that kind
Our rustic garden's barren; and I care not
To get slips of them.

85 *Polixenes.*   Wherefore, gentle maiden,
Do you neglect them?

Perdita.   For I have heard it said,
There is an art, which in their piedness shares
With great creating Nature.

Polixenes.   Say there be;
Yet Nature is made better by no mean
90 But Nature makes that mean; so over that art,
Which you say adds to Nature, is an art,
That Nature makes. You see, sweet maid, we marry
A gentler scion to the wildest stock,
And make conceive a bark of baser kind
95 By bud of nobler race. This is an art

---

75 *Seeming and savor* color and scent   76 *Grace and remembrance* (rue is for grace and repentance; rosemary for remembrance, because the fragrance lasted indefinitely)   82 *gillyvors* pinks (sometimes in modern regional usage, "wallflowers"; but here Perdita means carnations, pinks, sweet william—the blooms have streaks of color, and for this reason were associated with loose women. The whole debate on the gillyvors is discussed in the Introduction)   83 *Nature's bastards* (see Introduction)

Which does mend Nature, change it rather; but
The art itself is Nature.°

Perdita.   So it is.

Polixenes. Then make your garden rich in gillyvors,
And do not call them bastards.

Perdita.   I'll not put
The dibble° in earth, to set one slip of them;   *100*
No more than were I painted, I would wish
This youth should say 'twere well, and only therefore
Desire to breed by me. Here's flow'rs for you:
Hot lavender,° mints, savory, marjoram,
The marigold that goes to bed wi' th' sun,   *105*
And with him rises, weeping; these are flow'rs
Of middle summer, and I think they are given
To men of middle age. You're very welcome.

Camillo. I should leave grazing, were I of your flock,
And only live by gazing.

Perdita.   Out, alas!   *110*
You'd be so lean that blasts of January
Would blow you through and through. [*To Florizel*]
     Now, my fair'st friend,
I would I had some flow'rs o' th' spring, that might
Become your time of day—[*to Shepherdesses*] and
     yours, and yours,
That wear upon your virgin branches yet   *115*
Your maidenheads growing. O Proserpina,
For the flow'rs now, that, frighted, thou let'st fall
From Dis's wagon!° Daffodils,
That come before the swallow dares, and take°
The winds of March with beauty; violets, dim,   *120*
But sweeter than the lids of Juno's eyes,

89-97 *Yet Nature is made . . . itself is Nature* (see Introduction)
100 *dibble* tool for making holes to plant seeds or cuttings   104 *Hot lavender* (the epithet has not been satisfactorily explained)   116-18 *Proserpina . . . Dis's wagon* (the God of the Underworld bore off Proserpina as she gathered flowers with her mother, Ceres, in the Vale of Enna. Ovid's account [*Metamorphoses* V.398-99] mentions that she dropped the flowers she had picked)   119 *take* charm, captivate

Or Cytherea's° breath; pale primroses,
That die unmarried° ere they can behold
Bright Phoebus in his strength (a malady
125   Most incident to maids); bold oxlips, and
The crown imperial; lilies of all kinds,
The flower-de-luce being one. O, these I lack
To make you garlands of, and my sweet friend,
To strew him o'er and o'er!

Florizel.   What, like a corse?°

130 *Perdita.* No, like a bank for Love to lie and play on;
Not like a corse; or if, not to be buried,
But quick° and in mine arms. Come, take your
    flow'rs;
Methinks I play as I have seen them do
In Whitsun pastorals;° sure this robe of mine
Does change my disposition.

135 *Florizel.*   What you do
Still betters what is done. When you speak, sweet,
I'd have you do it ever; when you sing,
I'd have you buy and sell so; so give alms,
Pray so; and for the ord'ring your affairs,
140   To sing them too. When you do dance, I wish you
A wave o' th' sea, that you might ever do
Nothing but that—move still, still so,
And own no other function. Each your doing,
So singular in each particular,
145   Crowns what you are doing in the present deeds,
That all your acts are queens.°

Perdita.   O Doricles,°
Your praises are too large; but that your youth
And the true blood which peeps° fairly through 't,

---

122 *Cytherea's* Venus'   123 *die unmarried* (because it grows in shade,
and in spring, Milton has "the rathe primrose that forsaken dies")
129 *corse* corpse   132 *quick* alive   134 *Whitsun pastorals* (Whitsun was
the season for games related to old spring festivals, and Perdita refers
probably to the King and Queen in these games—identified with Robin
Hood and Marian)   143-46 *Each your doing . . . queens* "Your manner in each act crowns the act" (Dr. Johnson)   146 *Doricles* (Florizel's
pseudonym)   148 *peeps* shows

Do plainly give you out an unstained shepherd,
With wisdom I might fear, my Doricles,   *150*
You wooed me the false way.°

Florizel.   I think you have
As little skill° to fear, as I have purpose
To put you to 't. But come, our dance, I pray;
Your hand, my Perdita; so turtles° pair
That never mean to part.

Perdita.   I'll swear for 'em.   *155*

Polixenes. This is the prettiest low-born lass that ever
Ran on the greensward; nothing she does or seems
But smacks of something greater than herself,
Too noble for this place.

Camillo.   He tells her something
That makes her blood look out;° good sooth° she
   is   *160*
The queen of curds and cream.°

Clown.   Come on, strike up.

Dorcas. Mopsa must be your mistress; marry, garlic
To mend her kissing with!°

Mopsa.   Now, in good time!°

Clown. Not a word, a word, we stand upon our manners.
Come, strike up.   *165*

   Here a dance of Shepherds and Shepherdesses.

Polixenes. Pray, good shepherd, what fair swain is this,
Which dances with your daughter?

Shepherd. They call him Doricles, and boasts himself
To have a worthy feeding;° but I have it

151 *the false way* i.e., by flattery   152 *skill* reason   154 *turtles* doves
160 *blood look out* blush   160 *good sooth* in truth   161 *queen of curds
and cream* (J. D. Wilson argues that Camillo is calling Perdita a "white-
pot queen"—the name given in some May games to the queen, by association with a dish called "white-pot," made of custard, cream, spices,
apples, etc.)   162-63 *garlic . . . kissing with* use garlic to overcome her
bad breath   163 *in good time* (expression of indignation)   169 *feeding*
landed property

170   Upon his own report, and I believe it:
      He looks like sooth. He says he loves my daughter;
      I think so too; for never gazed the moon
      Upon the water, as he'll stand and read,
      As 'twere, my daughter's eyes; and, to be plain,
175   I think there is not half a kiss to choose
      Who loves another° best.

Polixenes.   She dances featly.°

Shepherd. So she does anything, though I report it
      That should be silent. If young Doricles
      Do light upon her, she shall bring him that
180   Which he not dreams of.

                Enter Servant.

Servant. O master, if you did but hear the peddler at
      the door, you would never dance again after a
      tabor° and pipe; no, the bagpipe could not move
      you. He sings several tunes faster than you'll tell°
185   money; he utters them as he had eaten ballads,°
      and all men's ears grew to his tunes.

Clown. He could never come better; he shall come in;
      I love a ballad but even too well, if it be doleful
      matter merrily set down; or a very pleasant thing
190   indeed, and sung lamentably.

Servant. He hath songs for man or woman of all
      sizes; no milliner can so fit his customers with gloves.
      He has the prettiest love songs for maids, so without
      bawdry, which is strange; with such delicate bur-
195   dens° of dildos and fadings:° "Jump her, and thump
      her";° and where some stretch-mouthed rascal
      would, as it were, mean mischief, and break a foul
      gap° into the matter, he makes the maid to answer,

---

¹⁷⁶ *another* the other   ¹⁷⁶ *featly* nimbly   ¹⁸³ *tabor* little drum   ¹⁸⁴ *tell*
count   ¹⁸⁵ *ballads* broadsheet words and music, to familiar tunes and on
topical subjects   ¹⁹⁴⁻⁹⁵ *burdens* refrains   ¹⁹⁵ *dildos and fadings* (dildos,
often mentioned in ballad refrains, are phalli; fadings are indecent refrains)   ¹⁹⁵⁻⁹⁶ *Jump her and thump her* (familiar ballad refrains)
¹⁹⁷⁻⁹⁸ *foul gap* i.e., a break in the song for obscene patter

"Whoop, do me no harm, good man";° puts him
off, slights him, with "Whoop, do me no harm, good   200
man."

Polixenes. This is a brave fellow.

Clown. Believe me, thou talkest of an admirable
conceited° fellow. Has he any unbraided° wares?

Servant. He hath ribbons of all the colors i' th' rain-   205
bow; points,° more than all the lawyers in Bohemia
can learnedly handle, though they come to him
by th' gross;° inkles,° caddisses,° cambrics, lawns.
Why, he sings 'em over, as they were gods or
goddesses; you would think a smock were a she-   210
angel, he so chants to the sleevehand,° and the
work about the square° on 't.

Clown. Prithee bring him in, and let him approach
singing.

Perdita. Forewarn him that he use no scurrilous words   215
in 's tunes.

                        [Exit Servant.]

Clown. You have of these peddlers° that have more
in them than you'd think, sister.

Perdita. Ay, good brother, or go about to° think.

              Enter Autolycus, singing.

     Lawn as white as driven snow,   220
     Cypress° black as e'er was crow,
     Gloves as sweet as damask roses,°
     Masks for faces, and for noses;°

---

199 *Whoop ... good man* (an extant ballad, coarse in character, has this
refrain. The joke in this speech lies in the servant's praising Autolycus
for the decency of his songs, and simultaneously betraying the fact of
their indecency) 204 *conceited* witty 204 *unbraided* new ("braided wares"
are shop-soiled) 206 *points* tagged laces, by which clothes were held up
(with a pun on the sense of "arguments") 208 *gross* twelve dozen points
(also with reference to clerkly "engrossing," the lawyer's fair copying)
208 *inkles* linen tapes 208 *caddisses* worsted tapes for garters 211 *sleevehand* cuff 212 *square* embroidered yoke 217 *You have of these peddlers* there are peddlers 219 *go about to* intend to 221 *Cypress* crape
222 *Gloves ... roses* (it was the fashion to perfume gloves) 223 *Masks
... noses* (to protect ladies' faces or noses from the sun)

Bugle-bracelet,° necklace-amber,
225 Perfume for a lady's chamber;
Golden quoifs° and stomachers
For my lads to give their dears;
Pins and poking-sticks° of steel;
What maids lack from head to heel!
230 Come buy of me, come, come buy, come buy,
Buy lads, or else your lasses cry; come buy!

Clown. If I were not in love with Mopsa, thou shouldst take no money of me; but being enthralled as I am, it will also be the bondage° of certain ribbons
235 and gloves.

Mopsa. I was promised them against° the feast, but they come not too late now.

Dorcas. He hath promised you more than that, or there be liars.

240 *Mopsa.* He hath paid you all he promised you; may be he has paid you more, which will shame you to give him again.°

Clown. Is there no manners left among maids? Will they wear their plackets° where they should bear
245 their faces? Is there not milking-time, when you are going to bed, or kiln-hole,° to whistle of these secrets, but you must be tittle-tattling before all our guests? 'Tis well they are whis'pring. Clammer° your tongues, and not a word more.

---

²²⁴ *Bugle-bracelet* bracelet of beads   ²²⁶ *quoifs* head scarves   ²²⁸ *poking-sticks* metal rods used in ironing starched ruffs   ²³⁴ *bondage* i.e., he is a prisoner of Mopsa, and will take the fairings into captivity with him   ²³⁶ *against* before   ²⁴¹⁻⁴² *paid you more . . . give him again* (this girlish insult means: "Perhaps he has made you pregnant")   ²⁴⁴ *plackets* petticoats, or slits in petticoats (often used indecently. Here the Clown merely means that they should not as it were wash their dirty linen in public)   ²⁴⁶ *kiln-hole* the place containing the fire for malt making (convenient for confidential talk)   ²⁴⁸ *Clammer* silence (technical term in bellringing)

Mopsa. I have done. Come, you promised me a   250
tawdry-lace,° and a pair of sweet gloves.

Clown. Have I not told thee how I was cozened by the
way, and lost all my money?

Autolycus. And indeed, sir, there are cozeners abroad;
therefore it behooves men to be wary.   255

Clown. Fear not thou, man; thou shalt lose nothing
here.

Autolycus. I hope so, sir, for I have about me many
parcels of charge.°

Clown. What hast here? Ballads?   260

Mopsa. Pray now, buy some. I love a ballad in print,
a-life,° for then we are sure they are true.

Autolycus. Here's one to a very doleful tune, how a
usurer's wife was brought to bed of twenty money-
bags at a burden, and how she longed to eat adders'   265
heads and toads carbonadoed.°

Mopsa. Is it true, think you?

Autolycus. Very true, and but a month old.

Dorcas. Bless me from marrying a usurer!

Autolycus. Here's the midwife's name to 't: one Mis-   270
tress Taleporter, and five or six honest wives that
were present. Why should I carry lies abroad?

Mopsa. Pray you now, buy it.

Clown. Come on, lay it by, and let's first see moe°
ballads; we'll buy the other things anon.   275

Autolycus. Here's another ballad, of a fish° that appeared upon the coast on Wednesday the fourscore of April, forty thousand fathom above water,
and sung this ballad against the hard hearts of

---

²⁵¹ *tawdry-lace* silk worn around the neck (called after St. Audrey
[Ethelreda], who was punished for youthful ostentation—especially fine
necklaces—by a tumor in the throat)   ²⁵⁹ *parcels of charge* goods of
value   ²⁶² *a-life* dearly   ²⁶⁶ *carbonadoed* cut up and broiled   ²⁷⁴ *moe*
more   ²⁷⁶ *of a fish* (records of very similar ballads survive)

280   maids; it was thought she was a woman, and was
turned into a cold fish for she would not exchange
flesh with one that loved her. The ballad is very
pitiful, and as true.

Dorcas. Is it true too, think you?

285 *Autolycus.* Five justices' hands at it, and witnesses
more than my pack will hold.

Clown. Lay it by too; another.

Autolycus. This is a merry ballad, but a very pretty
one.

290 *Mopsa.* Let's have some merry ones.

Autolycus. Why, this is a passing merry one, and goes
to the tune of "Two Maids Wooing a Man." There's
scarce a maid westward but she sings it; 'tis in
request, I can tell you.

295 *Mopsa.* We can both sing it. If thou 'lt bear a part, thou
shalt hear; 'tis in three parts.

Dorcas. We had the tune on 't, a month ago.

Autolycus. I can bear my part, you must know 'tis
my occupation. Have at it with you.

Song.

300 *Autolycus.*   Get you hence, for I must go
                    Where it fits not you to know.

    Dorcas.   Whither?

    Mopsa.   O whither?

    Dorcas.   Whither?

305 *Mopsa.*   It becomes thy oath full well,
                    Thou to me thy secrets tell.

    Dorcas.   Me too; let me go thither.

    Mopsa.   Or thou go'st to th' grange or mill,

    Dorcas.   If to either thou dost ill.

310 *Autolycus.*   Neither.

    Dorcas.   What, neither?

Autolycus.   Neither.

Dorcas.   Thou hast sworn my love to be.

Mopsa.   Thou hast sworn it more to me.
                   Then whither goest? Say, whither?   315

Clown. We'll have this song out anon by ourselves;
  my father and the gentlemen are in sad° talk, and
  we'll not trouble them. Come bring away thy pack
  after me; wenches, I'll buy for you both. Peddler,
  let's have the first choice; follow me, girls.   320

          [*Exeunt Clown, Dorcas, and Mopsa.*]

Autolycus. And you shall pay well for 'em.

                    Song.

   Will you buy any tape, or lace for your cape,
      My dainty duck, my dear-a?
   Any silk, any thread, any toys for your head,
      Of the new'st, and fin'st fin'st wear-a?   325
   Come to the peddler, money's a meddler,
      That doth utter° all men's ware-a.

                              Exit.

               Enter Servant.

Servant. Master, there is three carters, three shepherds,
  three neatherds,° three swineherds that have
  made themselves all men of hair;° they call them-   330
  selves saltiers,° and they have a dance, which the
  wenches say is a gallimaufry° of gambols, because
  they are not in 't; but they themselves are o' th'
  mind, if it be not too rough for some that know
  little but bowling,° it will please plentifully.   335

Shepherd. Away! We'll none on 't; here has been too
  much homely foolery already. I know, sir, we weary
  you.

Polixenes. You weary those that refresh us; pray let's
  see these four threes of herdsmen.

---

³¹⁷ *sad* serious   ³²⁷ *utter* put forth   ³²⁹ *neatherds* cowherds   ³³⁰ *men
of hair* hairy men, satyrs (or the wild men of medieval art and entertainment)   ³³¹ *saltiers,* satyrs (or perhaps leapers, vaulters, from Fr. *saultier,*
"vaulter")   ³³² *gallimaufry* hodgepodge   ³³⁵ *bowling* (here, a gentle
activity, contrasted with the acrobatic dance)

340　*Servant.* One three of them, by their own report, sir,
　　　hath danced before the King;° and not the worst
　　　of the three but jumps twelve foot and a half by
　　　th' squier.°

　　　Shepherd. Leave your prating; since these good men
345　are pleased, let them come in; but quickly now.

　　　Servant. Why, they stay at door, sir.　　　　[*Exit.*]

　　　　　　Here a dance of twelve Satyrs.

　　　Polixenes. [*To Shepherd*] O father, you'll know more
　　　of that hereafter.
　　　　[*To Camillo*] Is it not too far gone? 'Tis time to part
　　　them.
　　　He's simple and tells much. How now, fair shep-
　　　herd!
350　Your heart is full of something that does take
　　　Your mind from feasting. Sooth, when I was young,
　　　And handed° love as you do, I was wont
　　　To load my she with knacks; I would have ransacked
　　　The peddler's silken treasury, and have poured it
355　To her acceptance: you have let him go,
　　　And nothing marted with° him. If your lass
　　　Interpretation should abuse,° and call this
　　　Your lack of love or bounty, you were straited°
　　　For a reply, at least if you make a care
　　　Of happy holding her.

360　*Florizel.*　　　　　　Old sir, I know
　　　She prizes not such trifles as these are;
　　　The gifts she looks from me are packed and locked
　　　Up in my heart, which I have given already,
　　　But not delivered.° O, hear me breathe my life
365　Before this ancient sir, who, it should seem,
　　　Hath sometime loved: I take thy hand, this hand
　　　As soft as dove's down, and as white as it,

---

341 *before the King* (the performer of this dance had certainly done so,
perhaps in this very dance)　343 *squier* rule　352 *handed* dealt with
356 *marted with* bought of　357 *Interpretation should abuse* choose to
misunderstand　358 *straited* in difficulties　363-64 *given . . . delivered*
the deal is settled, but the goods not yet handed over

Or Ethiopian's tooth, or the fanned snow that's
  bolted°
By th' northern blasts twice o'er——

Polixenes.   What follows
  this?
How prettily th' young swain seems to wash   370
The hand was fair° before! I have put you out;
But to your protestation: let me hear
What you profess.

Florizel.   Do, and be witness to 't.

Polixenes. And this my neighbor too?

Florizel.   And he, and more
Than he, and men; the earth, the heavens, and all: 375
That were I crowned the most imperial monarch,
Thereof most worthy; were I the fairest youth
That ever made eye swerve; had force and knowl-
  edge
More than was ever man's, I would not prize them
Without her love; for her, employ them all,   380
Commend them, and condemn them to her service,
Or to their own perdition.°

Polixenes.   Fairly offered.

Camillo. This shows a sound affection.

Shepherd.   But, my daughter,
Say you the like to him?

Perdita.   I cannot speak
So well, nothing so well; no, nor mean better.   385
By th' pattern of mine own thoughts I cut out
The purity of his.

Shepherd.   Take hands, a bargain;
And friends unknown, you shall bear witness to 't:
I give my daughter to him, and will make
Her portion equal his.

Florizel.   O, that must be   390

---

[368] *bolted* sifted   [371] *was fair* that was fair   [381-82] *Commend . . . per-dition* commend them to her service, or condemn them to their own perdition

I' th' virtue of your daughter. One being dead,
I shall have more than you can dream of yet,
Enough then for your wonder.° But come on,
Contract us 'fore these witnesses.

Shepherd.   Come, your hand;
And, daughter, yours.

395 *Polixenes.*   Soft, swain, awhile, beseech you,
Have you a father?

Florizel.   I have; but what of him?

Polixenes. Knows he of this?

Florizel.   He neither does, nor shall.

Polixenes. Methinks a father
Is at the nuptial of his son a guest
400 That best becomes the table. Pray you once more,
Is not your father grown incapable
Of reasonable affairs? Is he not stupid
With age and alt'ring rheums?° Can he speak, hear?
Know man from man? Dispute his own estate?
405 Lies he not bed-rid? And again does nothing
But what he did being childish?

Florizel.   No, good sir;
He has his health, and ampler strength indeed
Than most have of his age.

Polixenes.   By my white beard,
You offer him, if this be so, a wrong
410 Something unfilial. Reason my son°
Should choose himself a wife, but as good reason
The father, all whose joy is nothing else
But fair posterity, should hold some counsel
In such a business.

Florizel.   I yield all this;
415 But for some other reasons, my grave sir,
Which 'tis not fit you know, I not acquaint

392–93 *I shall have more . . . your wonder* I shall have more than you
can at this time dream of, and enough to amaze you when you know of
it   403 *alt'ring rheums* i.e., rheumatic afflictions which disturb his judgment   410 *Reason my son* there is reason that my son

My father of this business.

Polixenes.   Let him know 't.

Florizel. He shall not.

Polixenes.   Prithee, let him.

Florizel.   No, he must not.

Shepherd. Let him, my son; he shall not need to grieve
   At knowing of thy choice.

Florizel.   Come, come, he must not.   420
   Mark our contract.°

Polixenes. [*Discovering himself*] Mark your divorce,
      young sir,
   Whom son I dare not call; thou art too base
   To be acknowledged. Thou, a scepter's heir,
   That thus affect'st° a sheep-hook! Thou, old traitor,
   I am sorry that by hanging thee, I can   425
   But shorten thy life one week. And thou, fresh piece
   Of excellent witchcraft, who of force must know
   The royal fool thou cop'st with——

Shepherd.   O my heart!

Polixenes. I'll have thy beauty scratched with briers
      and made
   More homely than thy state. For thee, fond boy,   430
   If I may ever know thou dost but sigh
   That thou no more shalt see this knack—as never
   I mean thou shalt—we'll bar thee from succession;
   Not hold thee of our blood, no not our kin,
   Farre than Deucalion off.° Mark thou my words.   435
   Follow us to the court. Thou, churl, for this time,
   Though full of our displeasure, yet we free thee
   From the dead blow of it. And you, enchantment,

---

⁴²¹ *contract* (J. D. Wilson in the New Cambridge edition points out
that "we have here a description, all but the final solemn words, of one
of those betrothal ceremonies which were held as legally binding as
marriage in church")   ⁴²⁴ *affect'st* desirest, lovest   ⁴³⁵ *Farre than
Deucalion off* further back than Deucalion (legendary ancient king of
Thessaly)

Worthy enough a herdsman—yea him, too,

440   That makes himself, but for our honor therein,
Unworthy thee° —if ever henceforth thou
These rural latches to his entrance open,
Or hoop his body more with thy embraces,
I will devise a death as cruel for thee
As thou art tender to 't.   *Exit.*

445 *Perdita.*   Even here undone!
I was not much afeard; for once or twice
I was about to speak and tell him plainly,
The selfsame sun that shines upon his court
Hides not his visage from our cottage, but
Looks on alike. [*To Florizel*] Will 't please you, sir,

450   be gone?
I told you what would come of this. Beseech you,
Of your own state take care: this dream of mine
Being now awake, I'll queen it no inch farther,
But milk my ewes, and weep.

    Camillo.   Why, how now, father!
Speak ere thou diest.

455 *Shepherd.*   I cannot speak nor think,
Nor dare to know that which I know. [*To Florizel*]
        O sir,
You have undone a man of fourscore three,
That thought to fill his grave in quiet, yea,
To die upon the bed my father died,

460   To lie close by his honest bones; but now
Some hangman must put on my shroud, and lay me
Where no priest shovels in dust.° Oh cursèd wretch,
That knew'st this was the Prince, and wouldst
        adventure
To mingle faith with him! Undone, undone!

465   If I might die within this hour, I have lived
To die when I desire.   *Exit.*

    Florizel.   Why look you so upon me?

439-41 *yea him . . . Unworthy thee* indeed, you're worthy of Florizel—
whose conduct has made him, save for the fact of his being my son,
unworthy of you   462 *Where no priest shovels in dust* (before the Ref-
ormation, and even in the First Prayer Book of Edward VI, the priest
was directed to do this. Felons were buried by the gallows)

I am but sorry, not afeard; delayed,
But nothing altered. What I was, I am;
More straining on, for plucking back; not following
My leash unwillingly.°

Camillo.   Gracious my lord,   470
You know your father's temper; at this time
He will allow no speech—which I do guess
You do not purpose to him—and as hardly
Will he endure your sight as yet, I fear;
Then, till the fury of his Highness settle,   475
Come not before him.

Florizel.   I not purpose it.
I think, Camillo?

Camillo.   Even he, my lord.

Perdita. How often have I told you 'twould be thus?
How often said my dignity would last
But till 'twere known?

Florizel.   It cannot fail, but by   480
The violation of my faith, and then
Let Nature crush the sides o' th' earth together,
And mar the seeds within.° Lift up thy looks;
From my succession wipe me, father, I
Am heir to my affection.

Camillo.   Be advised.   485

Florizel. I am, and by my fancy; if my reason
Will thereto be obedient, I have reason;
If not, my senses better pleased with madness,°
Do bid it welcome.

Camillo.   This is desperate, sir.

⁴⁶⁹⁻⁷⁰ *More straining on . . . unwillingly* (the image is of a hound.
Florizel continues on his chosen course, all the more strongly for
having been dragged back; he is not going to do as his father says
against his will)   ⁴⁸²⁻⁸³ *Let Nature . . . the seeds within* (for this image
of the end of creation compare *Macbeth* IV.i.59 and *Lear* III.ii.8)
⁴⁸⁶⁻⁸⁸ *fancy . . . reason . . . madness* if the fancy, which makes images,
is not obedient to the reason—a higher mental power—the result is madness or dream (Florizel wants his reason to obey his fancy; otherwise,
he says, he'd rather be mad. For the psychology involved, see *Midsummer Night's Dream* V.i.2 ff.)

490 *Florizel.* So call it, but it does fulfill my vow;
　　　I needs must think it honesty. Camillo,
　　　Not for Bohemia, nor the pomp that may
　　　Be thereat gleaned; for all the sun sees or
　　　The close earth wombs or the profound seas hide
495　In unknown fathoms, will I break my oath
　　　To this my fair beloved. Therefore, I pray you,
　　　As you have ever been my father's honored friend,
　　　When he shall miss me, as in faith I mean not
　　　To see him any more, cast your good counsels
500　Upon his passion; let myself and Fortune
　　　Tug° for the time to come. This you may know,
　　　And so deliver: I am put to sea
　　　With her whom here I cannot hold on shore;
　　　And most opportune° to her need, I have
505　A vessel rides fast by, but not prepared
　　　For this design. What course I mean to hold
　　　Shall nothing benefit your knowledge, nor
　　　Concern me the reporting.

　　Camillo.　　　　　　　　O my lord,
　　　I would your spirit were easier for advice,
　　　Or stronger for your need.

510 *Florizel.*　　　　　　　Hark, Perdita——
　　　[*To Camillo*] I'll hear you by and by.

　　Camillo.　　　　　　　　He's irremovable,
　　　Resolved for flight. Now were I happy if
　　　His going I could frame to serve my turn,
　　　Save him from danger, do him love and honor,
515　Purchase the sight again of dear Sicilia,
　　　And that unhappy king, my master, whom
　　　I so much thirst to see.

　　Florizel.　　　　　　　Now, good Camillo,
　　　I am so fraught with curious° business that
　　　I leave out ceremony.°

　　Camillo.　　　　　　Sir, I think

501 *Tug* contend, strive　504 *opportune* (accent on second syllable)
518 *curious* needing great care　519 *ceremony* (Florizel is apologizing
for having broken away from Camillo to hold his urgent private talk
with Perdita)

You have heard of my poor services i' th' love   520
That I have borne your father?

Florizel.   Very nobly
Have you deserved; it is my father's music
To speak your deeds, not little of his care
To have them recompensed, as thought on.

Camillo.   Well, my lord,
If you may please to think I love the King,   525
And through him what's nearest to him, which is
Your gracious self, embrace but my direction,°
If your more ponderous and settled project
May suffer alteration. On mine honor,
I'll point you where you shall have such receiving   530
As shall become your Highness, where you may
Enjoy your mistress; from the whom, I see
There's no disjunction to be made, but by—
As heavens forfend—your ruin; marry her;
And with my best endeavors, in your absence,   535
Your discontenting° father strive to qualify°
And bring him up to liking.

Florizel.   How, Camillo,
May this, almost a miracle, be done?
That I may call thee something more than man,
And after that trust to thee.

Camillo.   Have you thought on   540
A place whereto you'll go?

Florizel.   Not any yet;
But as th' unthought-on accident is guilty
To what we wildly do, so we profess
Ourselves to be the slaves of chance, and flies
Of every wind that blows.°

Camillo.   Then list° to me.   545
This follows, if you will not change your purpose,

---

527 *direction* advice 536 *discontenting* displeased 536 *qualify* appease,
moderate (used, for example, of tempering wine with water)
542–45 *But as . . . wind that blows* since we are compelled to this wild
behavior by a chance we never foresaw, we think of ourselves as the
slaves of chance, and will go where it sends us, like flies in a wind
545 *list* listen

But undergo this flight: make for Sicilia,
And there present yourself and your fair princess
(For so I see she must be) 'fore Leontes.
550 She shall be habited as it becomes
The partner of your bed. Methinks I see
Leontes opening his free arms and weeping
His welcomes forth; asks thee, the son, forgiveness,
As 'twere i' th' father's person; kisses the hands
555 Of your fresh princess; o'er and o'er divides him
'Twixt his unkindness and his kindness: th' one
He chides to hell, and bids the other grow
Faster° than thought or time.

Florizel.   Worthy Camillo,
What color° for my visitation shall I
Hold up before him?

560 *Camillo.*   Sent by the King your father
To greet him, and to give him comforts. Sir,
The manner of your bearing towards him, with
What you, as from your father, shall deliver,
Things known betwixt us three, I'll write you down,
565 The which shall point you forth at every sitting
What you must say, that he shall not perceive,
But that° you have your father's bosom there,
And speak his very heart.

Florizel.   I am bound to you;
There is some sap° in this.

Camillo.   A course more promising
570 Than a wild dedication of yourselves
To unpathed waters, undreamed shores, most cer-
tain
To miseries enough: no hope to help you,
But as you shake off one, to take another;
Nothing so certain as your anchors, who
575 Do their best office if they can but stay° you,
Where you'll be loath to be. Besides, you know,
Prosperity's the very bond of love,

Whose fresh complexion and whose heart together
Affliction alters.

Perdita.   One of these is true:
  I think affliction may subdue the cheek,   *580*
  But not take in the mind.

Camillo.   Yea? Say you so?
  There shall not at your father's house these seven
    years°
  Be born another such.

Florizel.   My good Camillo,
  She is as forward of her breeding as
  She is i' th' rear 'our birth.°

Camillo.   I cannot say 'tis pity   *585*
  She lacks instructions, for she seems a mistress
  To most that teach.

Perdita.   Your pardon, sir; for this,
  I'll blush you thanks.

Florizel.   My prettiest Perdita!
  But O, the thorns we stand upon! Camillo—
  Preserver of my father, now of me,   *590*
  The medicine° of our house—how shall we do?
  We are not furnished like Bohemia's son,
  Nor shall appear° in Sicilia.

Camillo.   My lord,
  Fear none of this. I think you know my fortunes
  Do all lie there; it shall be so my care   *595*
  To have you royally appointed,° as if
  The scene you play were mine. For instance, sir,
  That you may know you shall not want—one word.
                    [They talk aside.]

          Enter Autolycus.

Autolycus. Ha, ha, what a fool° Honesty is! And

582 *these seven years* (used to signify a long, indefinite period)
584–85 *She is as forward . . . our birth* she is as far in advance of the way
of life she was reared to as she is inferior to us in birth   591 *medicine*
physician   593 *appear* appear so (the second word may have dropped
out)   596 *royally appointed* equipped like a prince   599 *Ha, ha, what
a fool . . .* (these lines echo passages in Greene's *Second Part of
Conny-catching* [1592]. The character of Autolycus, and the account of
the tricks of his trade, is indebted to this book)

600 Trust, his sworn brother, a very simple gentleman. I
have sold all my trumpery: not a counterfeit stone,
not a ribbon, glass, pomander, brooch, table-book,°
ballad, knife, tape, glove, shoe-tie, bracelet, horn-
ring, to keep my pack from fasting. They throng
605 who should buy first, as if my trinkets had been
hallowed,° and brought a benediction to the buyer;
by which means I saw whose purse was best in picture,° and what I saw to my good use I remembered. My clown, who wants but something to be
610 a reasonable man, grew so in love with the wenches'
song, that he would not stir his pettitoes° till he had
both tune and words, which so drew the rest of the
herd to me that all their other senses stuck in ears:
you might have pinched a placket, it was senseless;
615 'twas nothing to geld a codpiece of a purse; I would
have filed keys off that hung in chains. No hearing,
no feeling, but my sir's° song, and admiring the
nothing° of it. So that in this time of lethargy I
picked and cut most of their festival purses; and had
620 not the old man come in with a hubbub against his
daughter and the King's son, and scared my
choughs° from the chaff, I had not left a purse
alive in the whole army.

[*Camillo, Florizel, and Perdita come forward.*]

Camillo. Nay, but my letters, by this means being there
625 So soon as you arrive, shall clear that doubt.

Florizel. And those that you'll procure from King
Leontes?

Camillo. Shall satisfy your father.

Perdita.   Happy be you!
All that you speak shows fair.

Camillo. [*Seeing Autolycus*] Who have we here?
We'll make an instrument of this, omit

602 *table-book* notebook   606 *hallowed* sacred   607–608 *in picture* to look
at (?)   611 *pettitoes* toes (especially of a pig)   617 *my sir's* the Clown's
618 *nothing* nothingness, nonsense (with perhaps, as Wilson suggests, a
pun on "noting")   622 *choughs* fools

Nothing may give us aid.   630

Autolycus. If they have overheard me now—why, hanging.

Camillo. How now, good fellow, why shak'st thou so? Fear not, man; here's no harm intended to thee.

Autolycus. I am a poor fellow, sir.

Camillo. Why, be so still; here's nobody will steal that 635 from thee. Yet for the outside of thy poverty we must make an exchange; therefore disease° thee instantly—thou must think there's a necessity in 't —and change garments with this gentleman; though the pennyworth on his side be the worst, yet hold 640 thee, there's some boot.° [*Giving money.*]

Autolycus. I am a poor fellow, sir. [*Aside*] I know ye well enough.

Camillo. Nay, prithee dispatch; the gentleman is half flayed° already.   645

Autolycus. Are you in earnest, sir? [*Aside*] I smell the trick on 't.

Florizel. Dispatch, I prithee.

Autolycus. Indeed, I have had earnest,° but I cannot with conscience take it.   650

Camillo. Unbuckle, unbuckle.

[*Florizel and Autolycus exchange garments.*]

Fortunate mistress—let my prophecy°
Come home to ye—you must retire yourself
Into some covert; take your sweetheart's hat
And pluck it o'er your brows, muffle your face,   655
Dismantle you, and, as you can, disliken
The truth of your own seeming,° that you may

---

637 *discase* undress   **641** *boot* extra reward   **645** *flayed* skinned (undressed)   **649** *earnest* money paid as installment, "deposit"   **652** *prophecy* (the prophecy is the form of address, "Fortunate mistress!")   **656-57** *disliken . . . seeming* (a complicated way of saying "alter your usual appearance," which may indicate Shakespeare's obsessive interest in problems related to "truth" and "seeming")

(For I do fear eyes over°) to shipboard
Get undescried.

Perdita. I see the play so lies
That I must bear a part.

660 *Camillo.* No remedy.
Have you done there?

Florizel. Should I now meet my father,
He would not call me son.

Camillo. Nay, you shall have no hat.
[*Giving hat to Perdita.*]

Come, lady, come; farewell, my friend.

Autolycus. Adieu, sir.

Florizel. O Perdita, what have we twain forgot?
665 Pray you, a word.

Camillo. [*Aside*] What I do next shall be to tell the
King
Of this escape, and whither they are bound;
Wherein my hope is, I shall so prevail
To force him after; in whose company
670 I shall re-view Sicilia, for whose sight
I have a woman's longing.

Florizel. Fortune speed us!
Thus we set on, Camillo, to th' seaside.

Camillo. The swifter speed, the better.

Exit [Camillo, with Florizel and Perdita].

Autolycus. I understand the business, I hear it. To have
675 an open ear, a quick eye, and a nimble hand, is
necessary for a cutpurse; a good nose is requisite
also, to smell out work for th' other senses. I see
this is the time that the unjust man doth thrive. What
an exchange had this been without boot! What a
680 boot is here, with this exchange! Sure, the gods do
this year connive at° us, and we may do anything

658 *eyes over* watching, spying eyes   681 *connive at* close their eyes to

extempore. The Prince himself is about a piece of
iniquity—stealing away from his father, with his
clog° at his heels; if I thought it were a piece of
honesty to acquaint the King withal, I would not   685
do 't. I hold it the more knavery to conceal it; and
therein am I constant to my profession.

Enter Clown and Shepherd.

Aside, aside! Here is more matter for a hot brain.
Every lane's end, every shop, church, session,
hanging, yields a careful man work.   690

Clown. See, see, what a man you are now! There is
no other way but to tell the King she's a changeling,
and none of your flesh and blood.

Shepherd. Nay, but hear me.

Clown. Nay, but hear me.   695

Shepherd. Go to, then.

Clown. She being none of your flesh and blood, your
flesh and blood has not offended the King, and so
your flesh and blood is not to be punished by him.
Show those things you found about her, those   700
secret things, all but what she has with her. This
being done, let the law go whistle; I warrant you.

Shepherd. I will tell the King all, every word, yea, and
his son's pranks too; who, I may say, is no honest
man, neither to his father nor to me, to go about to 705
make me the King's brother-in-law.

Clown. Indeed brother-in-law was the farthest off you
could have been to him; and then your blood had
been the dearer by I know not how much an ounce.

Autolycus. [*Aside*] Very wisely, puppies!   710

Shepherd. Well, let us to the King; there is that in this
fardel° will make him scratch his beard.

Autolycus. [*Aside*] I know not what impediment this
complaint may be to the flight of my master.

---

⁶⁸⁴ *clog* hindrance (Perdita)   ⁷¹² *fardel* bundle

715   *Clown.* Pray heartily he be at palace.°

     Autolycus. [*Aside*] Though I am not naturally honest,
       I am so sometimes by chance. Let me pocket up my
       peddler's excrement.° [*Takes off false beard.*] How
       now, rustics, whither are you bound?

720 *Shepherd.* To th' palace, an it like your worship.

     Autolycus. Your affairs there, what, with whom,° the
       condition of that fardel, the place of your dwelling,
       your names, your ages, of what having,° breeding,
       and anything that is fitting to be known, discover.

725 *Clown.* We are but plain fellows, sir.

     Autolycus. A lie: you are rough, and hairy. Let me
       have no lying; it becomes none but tradesmen, and
       they often give us soldiers the lie, but we pay them
       for it with stamped coin, not stabbing steel; there-
730   fore they do not give us the lie.°

     Clown. Your worship had like to have given us one,
       if you had not taken yourself with the manner.°

     Shepherd. Are you a courtier,° an 't like you, sir?

     Autolycus. Whether it like me or no, I am a courtier.
735   Seest thou not the air of the court in these enfold-
       ings? Hath not my gait in it the measure° of the
       court? Receives not thy nose court-odor from me?
       Reflect I not on thy baseness court-contempt?
       Think'st thou, for that I insinuate, or toaze° from
740   thee thy business, I am therefore no courtier? I am
       courtier cap-a-pé;° and one that will either push

---

715 *at palace* (the Clown speaks of the King being "at palace" as
he might of an ordinary man being "at home" [Cambridge editors])
718 *excrement* i.e., his false beard (hair, beard, and nails were called
"excrement," from L. *excrescere,* to grow out)   721 *what, with whom*
(parodying a form of legal questioning to terrify the rustics)   723 *having* property   727-30 *it becomes none . . . give us the lie* (tradesmen give the lie by giving short measure, but the simple soldier nevertheless pays them for the lie with money, not with his sword—so the
tradesmen are not, after all, *giving* the lie; they are selling it [J. D. Wilson's explanation])   732 *with the manner* in the act (at first Autolycus
was about to lie by saying "give" instead of "sell" when speaking of the
tradesmen; but he caught himself in the act and changed his statement)
733 *courtier* (Autolycus is wearing Florizel's festive clothes)   736 *measure* stately tread   739 *toaze* tease, worry, comb out   741 *cap-a-pé* head-
to-foot (of armor; here, thorough, complete)

on or pluck back thy business there; whereupon I
command thee to open thy affair.

Shepherd. My business, sir, is to the King.

Autolycus. What advocate hast thou to him?   745

Shepherd. I know not, an 't like you.

Clown. Advocate's the court-word for a pheasant;°
say you have none.

Shepherd. None, sir; I have no pheasant, cock nor hen.

Autolycus. How blessed are we that are not simple
men!   750
   Yet Nature might have made me as these are,
   Therefore I will not disdain.

Clown. This cannot be but a great courtier.

Shepherd. His garments are rich, but he wears them
not handsomely.   755

Clown. He seems to be the more noble in being fan-
tastical. A great man, I'll warrant; I know by the
picking on 's teeth.°

Autolycus. The fardel there? What's i' th' fardel?
Wherefore that box?   760

Shepherd. Sir, there lies such secrets in this fardel and
box, which none must know but the King, and which
he shall know within this hour, if I may come to th'
speech of him.

Autolycus. Age, thou hast lost thy labor.   765

Shepherd. Why, sir?

Autolycus. The King is not at the palace; he is gone
aboard a new ship, to purge melancholy and air
himself; for if thou be'st capable of things serious,
thou must know the King is full of grief.   770

Shepherd. So 'tis said, sir—about his son, that should
have married a shepherd's daughter.

Autolycus. If that shepherd be not in handfast,° let
him fly; the curses he shall have, the tortures he
shall feel, will break the back of man, the heart of   775
monster.

Clown. Think you so, sir?

⁷⁴⁷ *Advocate's . . . pheasant* (the Clown, misunderstanding the word,
thinks Autolycus is referring to the practice of bribing the judge with
a bird)   ⁷⁵⁸ *picking on 's teeth* (regarded as an elegant practice)
⁷⁷³ *handfast* custody

Autolycus. Not he alone shall suffer what wit can
make heavy, and vengeance bitter; but those that
780 are germane° to him, though removed fifty times,
shall all come under the hangman; which, though
it be great pity, yet it is necessary. An old sheep-
whistling rogue, a ram-tender, to offer to have his
daughter come into grace! Some say he shall be
785 stoned; but that death is too soft for him, say I.
Draw our throne into a sheepcote! All deaths are
too few, the sharpest too easy.

Clown. Has the old man e'er a son, sir, do you hear,
an 't like you, sir?

790 *Autolycus.* He has a son—who shall be flayed alive,
then 'nointed over with honey, set on the head of a
wasp's nest; then stand till he be three-quarters and a
dram dead; then recovered again with aqua-vitae or
some other hot infusion; then, raw as he is, and in
795 the hottest day prognostication° proclaims, shall he
be set against a brick wall, the sun looking with a
southward eye upon him, where he is to behold
him with flies blown to death. But what talk we of
these traitorly rascals, whose miseries are to be
800 smiled at, their offenses being so capital? Tell me,
for you seem to be honest plain men, what you have
to the King; being something gently considered,°
I'll bring you where he is aboard, tender° your
persons to his presence, whisper him in your be-
805 halfs; and if it be in man besides the King to effect
your suits, here is man shall do it.

Clown. He seems to be of great authority. Close with
him,° give him gold; and though authority be a
stubborn bear, yet he is oft led by the nose with
810 gold. Show the inside of your purse to the outside of
his hand, and no more ado. Remember—stoned,
and flayed alive.

Shepherd. An 't please you, sir, to undertake the busi-

---

780 *germane* related 795 *prognostication* weather forecast in the almanac
for the year 802 *being something gently considered* if you bribe me like
a gentleman (handsomely) 803 *tender* present 807-08 *Close with him*
accept his offer

ness for us, here is that gold I have; I'll make it as
much more, and leave this young man in pawn till *815*
I bring it you.

Autolycus. After I have done what I promised?

Shepherd. Ay, sir.

Autolycus. Well, give me the moiety.° Are you a
party in this business?   *820*

Clown. In some sort, sir; but though my case be a
pitful one, I hope shall not be flayed° out of it.

Autolycus. Oh, that's the case of the shepherd's son:
hang him, he'll be made an example.

Clown. Comfort, good comfort! We must to the King, *825*
and show our strange sights; he must know 'tis none
of your daughter, nor my sister; we are gone else.
Sir, I will give you as much as this old man does
when the business is performed, and remain, as he
says, your pawn till it be brought you.   *830*

Autolycus. I will trust you. Walk before toward the
seaside, go on the right hand; I will but look upon
the hedge,° and follow you.

Clown. We are blessed, in this man, as I may say, even
blessed.   *835*

Shepherd. Let's before, as he bids us. He was provided
to do us good.

                   [*Exeunt Shepherd and Clown.*]

Autolycus. If I had a mind to be honest, I see Fortune
would not suffer me: she drops booties in my mouth.
I am courted now with a double occasion—gold, *840*
and a means to do the Prince, my master, good;
which who knows how that may turn back° to my
advancement? I will bring these two moles, these
blind ones, aboard him. If he think it fit to shore
them again, and that the complaint they have to the *845*
King concerns him nothing, let him call me rogue
for being so far officious; for I am proof against that
title, and what shame else belongs to 't. To him will
I present them, there may be matter in it.   *Exit.*

· 819 *moiety* half 821–22 *caste . . . flayed* (punning on case/skin)
832–33 *look upon the hedge* i.e., relieve himself 842 *turn back* redound

ACT V

Scene I. [*Sicilia, the Court of Leontes.*]

Enter Leontes, Cleomenes, Dion, Paulina, Servants.

Cleomenes. Sir, you have done enough, and have per-
   formed
   A saintlike sorrow. No fault could you make
   Which you have not redeemed; indeed paid down
   More penitence than done trespass. At the last,
5 Do as the heavens have done: forget your evil;
   With them forgive yourself.

Leontes.   Whilst I remember
   Her and her virtues, I cannot forget
   My blemishes in them, and so still think of
   The wrong I did myself; which was so much,
10 That heirless it hath made my kingdom, and
   Destroyed the sweet'st companion that e'er man
   Bred his hopes out of.

Paulina.   True, too true, my lord.
   If one by one you wedded all the world,
   Or from the all that are took something good
15 To make a perfect woman, she you killed
   Would be unparalleled.

Leontes.   I think so. Killed?
   She I killed! I did so; but thou strik'st me
   Sorely, to say I did—it is as bitter
   Upon thy tongue as in my thought. Now, good now,
   Say so but seldom.

20 *Cleomenes.*   Not at all, good lady:

132

You might have spoken a thousand things that would
Have done the time more benefit, and graced°
Your kindness better.

Paulina.   You are one of those
Would have him wed again.

Dion.   If you would not so,
You pity not the state, nor the remembrance°   25
Of his most sovereign name; consider little
What dangers, by his Highness' fail° of issue,
May drop upon his kingdom, and devour
Incertain lookers-on.° What were more holy
Than to rejoice the former queen is well?   30
What holier than, for royalty's repair,
For present comfort, and for future good,
To bless the bed of majesty again
With a sweet fellow to 't?

Paulina.   There is none worthy,
Respecting her that's gone; besides, the gods   35
Will have fulfilled their secret purposes;
For has not the divine Apollo said—
Is 't not the tenor of his oracle—
That King Leontes shall not have an heir
Till his lost child be found? Which that it shall,   40
Is all as monstrous to our human reason
As my Antigonus to break his grave,
And come again to me; who, on my life,
Did perish with the infant. 'Tis your counsel
My lord should to the heavens be contrary,   45
Oppose against their wills. [*To Leontes*] Care not for issue,
The crown will find an heir. Great Alexander
Left his to th' worthiest: so his successor
Was like to be the best.

Leontes.   Good Paulina,
Who hast the memory of Hermione,   50

V.i.[22] *graced* suited   [25] *remembrance* (he means the perpetuation of the King's name in a son)   [27] *fail* failure   [29] *Incertain lookers-on* bystanders whose uncertainty makes them incapable of action

I know, in honor: O, that ever I
Had squared me to° thy counsel! Then, even now,
I might have looked upon my queen's full eyes,
Have taken treasure from her lips——

Paulina.   And left them
More rich for what they yielded.

55 *Leontes.*   Thou speak'st truth;
No more such wives, therefore no wife. One worse,
And better used, would make her sainted spirit
Again possess her corpse, and on this stage,
Where we offenders now appear,° soul-vexed,
And begin, "Why to me?"°

60 *Paulina.*   Had she such power,
She had just cause.

Leontes.   She had, and would incense me
To murder her I married.

Paulina.   I should so.
Were I the ghost that walked, I'd bid you mark
Her eye, and tell me for what dull part in 't
65 You chose her; then I'd shriek, that even your ears
Should rift to hear me, and the words that followed
Should be, "Remember mine."

Leontes.   Stars, stars,
And all eyes else, dead coals! Fear thou no wife;
I'll have no wife, Paulina.

Paulina.   Will you swear
70 Never to marry, but by my free leave?

Leontes. Never, Paulina, so be blessed my spirit.

Paulina. Then, good my lords, bear witness to his oath.

Cleomenes. You tempt him overmuch.

Paulina.   Unless another,

---

⁵² *squared me to* regulated myself by   ⁵⁹ *Where we offenders now appear*
(many attempts to emend this passage have given no better sense than
the Folio. The verb "appear" is needed both for the offenders and for
the ghost of Hermione; the obscurity arises from its doing duty for
both. Compare the famous difficulty in *Hamlet* IV.iv.53: "Rightly to be
great/Is not to stir without great argument . . . ," where "not" stands
for "not not")   ⁶⁰ *Why to me* Why do you offer such treatment to me

    As like Hermione as is her picture,
    Affront° his eye.

Cleomenes.   Good madam——

Paulina.   I have done;   75
    Yet if my lord will marry, if you will, sir—
    No remedy but you will—give me the office
    To choose you a queen; she shall not be so young
    As was your former, but she shall be such
    As, walked your first queen's ghost, it should take
      joy   80
    To see her in your arms.

Leontes.   My true Paulina,
    We shall not marry till thou bidd'st us.

Paulina.   That
    Shall be when your first queen's again in breath;
    Never till then.

               Enter a Servant.

Servant. One that gives out himself Prince Florizel,   85
    Son of Polixenes, with his princess—she
    The fairest I have yet beheld—desires access
    To your high presence.

Leontes.   What with him? He comes not
    Like to his father's greatness; his approach,
    So out of circumstance,° and sudden, tells us   90
    'Tis not a visitation framed,° but forced
    By need and accident. What train?°

Servant.   But few,
    And those but mean.

Leontes.   His princess, say you, with him?

Servant. Ay, the most peerless piece of earth, I think,
    That e'er the sun shone bright on.

Paulina.   O Hermione,   95
    As every present time doth boast itself
    Above a better, gone, so must thy grave

---

[75] *affront* confront [90] *out of circumstance* lacking ceremony [91] *framed*
planned [92] *train* attendants

Give way to what's seen now. Sir, you yourself
Have said, and writ so; but your writing now
100 Is colder than that theme:° "She had not been,
Nor was not to be equaled"; thus your verse°
Flowed with her beauty once; 'tis shrewdly ebbed,
To say you have seen a better.

Servant.   Pardon, madam:
The one I have almost forgot—your pardon—
105 The other, when she has obtained your eye,
Will have your tongue too. This is a creature,
Would she begin a sect, might quench the zeal
Of all professors° else; make proselytes
Of who she but bid follow.

Paulina.   How! Not women?

110 *Servant.* Women will love her that she is a woman
More worth than any man; men, that she is
The rarest of all women.

Leontes.   Go, Cleomenes,
Yourself, assisted with your honored friends,
Bring them to our embracement.
                              Exit [Cleomenes with others].
                                        Still, 'tis strange,
He should thus steal upon us.

115 *Paulina.*   Had our prince,
Jewel of children, seen this hour, he had paired
Well with this lord; there was not full a month
Between their births.

Leontes. Prithee no more; cease; thou know'st
120 He dies to me again, when talked of. Sure
When I shall see this gentleman, thy speeches
Will bring me to consider that which may
Unfurnish me of reason. They are come.

Enter Florizel, Perdita, Cleomenes, and others.

Your mother was most true to wedlock, Prince,

---

100 *theme* Hermione herself   101 *verse* (he had presumably written verses
of compliment to Hermione)   108 *professors* those who profess zeal for
religion (especially Puritans)

For she did print your royal father off,   *125*
Conceiving you. Were I but twenty-one,
Your father's image is so hit in you,
His very air, that I should call you brother,
As I did him, and speak of something wildly
By us performed before. Most dearly welcome!   *130*
And your fair princess—goddess! Oh, alas!
I lost a couple that 'twixt heaven and earth
Might thus have stood begetting wonder as
You, gracious couple, do. And then I lost—
All mine own folly—the society,   *135*
Amity too, of your brave father, whom,
Though bearing misery, I desire my life
Once more to look on him.°

Florizel.   By his command
Have I here touched Sicilia, and from him
Give you all greetings that a king, at friend,°   *140*
Can send his brother; and but infirmity,
Which waits upon worn times,° hath something
    seized°
His wished ability, he had himself
The lands and waters 'twixt your throne and his
Measured to look upon you; whom he loves   *145*
(He bade me say so) more than all the scepters
And those that bear them living.

Leontes.   Oh, my brother—
Good gentleman!—the wrongs I have done thee stir
Afresh within me; and these thy offices,°
So rarely kind, are as interpreters   *150*
Of my behindhand slackness.° Welcome hither,
As is the spring to th' earth! And hath he too
Exposed this paragon to th' fearful usage,
At least ungentle, of the dreadful Neptune,

136–38 *whom . . . on him* I wish to go on living, however miserably, in
order to look on him again (the final "him" is dispensable, but the
construction is not unique in Shakespeare) 140 *at friend* being in
friendship with 142 *worn times* advanced years 142 *seized* arrested
149 *offices* kindnesses, compliments 150–51 *interpreters . . . slackness*
put into words feelings I've been too slow in expressing

155   To greet a man not worth her pains, much less
        Th' adventure° of her person?

Florizel.   Good my lord,
        She came from Libya.

Leontes.   Where the warlike Smalus,
        That noble honored lord, is feared and loved?

Florizel. Most royal sir, from thence; from him, whose
            daughter
160   His tears proclaimed his, parting with her; thence,
        A prosperous south wind friendly, we have crossed,
        To execute the charge my father gave me,
        For visiting your Highness. My best train
        I have from your Sicilian shores dismissed;
165   Who for Bohemia bend, to signify
        Not only my success in Libya, sir,
        But my arrival and my wife's in safety
        Here where we are.

Leontes.   The blessèd gods
        Purge all infection from our air whilst you
170   Do climate° here! You have a holy father,
        A graceful° gentleman, against whose person,
        So sacred as it is, I have done sin;
        For which, the heavens, taking angry note,
        Have left me issueless; and your father's blessed,
175   As he from heaven merits it, with you,
        Worthy his goodness. What might I have been,
        Might I a son and daughter now have looked on,
        Such goodly things as you!

                        Enter a Lord.

Lord.   Most noble sir,
        That which I shall report will bear no credit,
180   Were not the proof so nigh. Please you, great sir,
        Bohemia greets you from himself, by me;
        Desires you to attach° his son, who has—
        His dignity and duty both cast off—

---

¹⁵⁶*adventure* risk   ¹⁷⁰*climate* reside   ¹⁷¹*graceful* virtuous   ¹⁸²*attach* arrest

Fled from his father, from his hopes, and with
A shepherd's daughter.

Leontes.   Where's Bohemia? Speak.   185

Lord. Here in your city; I now came from him.
I speak amazedly, and it becomes
My marvel° and my message. To your court
Whiles he was hast'ning—in the chase, it seems,
Of this fair couple—meets he on the way   190
The father of this seeming lady, and
Her brother, having both their country quitted,
With this young prince.

Florizel.   Camillo has betrayed me;
Whose honor and whose honesty till now
Endured all weathers.

Lord.   Lay 't so to his charge;   195
He's with the King your father.

Leontes.   Who? Camillo?

Lord. Camillo, sir; I spake with him; who now
Has these poor men in question.° Never saw I
Wretches so quake; they kneel, they kiss the earth;
Forswear° themselves as often as they speak.   200
Bohemia stops his ears, and threatens them
With divers deaths in death.°

Perdita.   Oh my poor father!
The heaven sets spies upon us, will not have
Our contract celebrated.

Leontes.   You are married?

Florizel. We are not, sir, nor are we like to be;   205
The stars, I see, will kiss the valleys first;
The odds for high and low 's alike.°

Leontes.   My lord,

187–88 *becomes/My marvel* suits my bewilderment   198 *in question*
in talk, in conference   200 *Forswear* deny on oath   202 *divers deaths
in death* various tortures   207 *The odds . . . alike* (dicing terms. "Fortune is a cheater who beguiles princes and shepherds alike with his false
dice" [J. D. Wilson])

Is this the daughter of a king?

Florizel.   She is,
When once she is my wife.

210 *Leontes.* That once, I see by your good father's speed,
Will come on very slowly. I am sorry,
Most sorry, you have broken from his liking,
Where you were tied in duty; and as sorry
Your choice is not so rich in worth° as beauty,
That you might well enjoy her.

215 *Florizel.*   Dear, look up.
Though Fortune, visible an enemy,
Should chase° us, with my father, power no jot
Hath she to change our loves. Beseech you, sir,
Remember since you owed no more to Time
220 Than I do now; with thought of such affections,
Step forth mine advocate; at your request
My father will grant precious things as trifles.

Leontes. Would he do so, I'd beg your precious mistress,
Which he counts but a trifle.

Paulina.   Sir, my liege,
225 Your eye hath too much youth in 't; not a month
'Fore your queen died, she was more worth such gazes
Than what you look on now.

Leontes.   I thought of her,
Even in these looks I made. But your petition
Is yet unanswered. I will to your father.
230 Your honor not o'erthrown by your desires,°
I am friend to them and you: upon which errand
I now go toward him. Therefore follow me,
And mark what way I make.° Come, good my lord.
                                        Exeunt.

---

214 *worth* rank   217 *chase* persecute   230 *Your honor . . . desires* (a
certain insistence on this point of prenuptial chastity is observable both
in this play and in *The Tempest*)   233 *what way I make* how far I
succeed

Scene II. [*Sicilia, before the palace of Leontes.*]

Enter Autolycus and a Gentleman.

Autolycus. Beseech you, sir, were you present at this
relation?

First Gentleman. I was by at the opening of the fardel,
heard the old shepherd deliver the manner how he
found it; whereupon, after a little amazedness, we   5
were all commanded out of the chamber; only this,
methought I heard the shepherd say, he found the
child.

Autolycus. I would most gladly know the issue of it.

First Gentleman. I make a broken delivery of the   10
business, but the changes I perceived in the King
and Camillo were very notes of admiration.° They
seemed almost, with staring on one another, to
tear the cases of their eyes.° There was speech in
their dumbness, language in their very gesture; they   15
looked as they had heard of a world ransomed, or
one destroyed. A notable passion of wonder appeared in them; but the wisest beholder that knew
no more but seeing° could not say if th' impor-
tance° were joy, or sorrow—but in the extremity   20
of the one it must needs be.

Enter another Gentleman.

Here comes a gentleman that happily° knows more:
the news, Rogero?

Second Gentleman. Nothing but bonfires. The oracle is
fulfilled; the King's daughter is found; such a deal   25

V.ii.¹² *notes of admiration* exclamation points   ¹⁴ *cases of their eyes*
eyelids   ¹⁹ *but seeing* but what he saw   ¹⁹⁻²⁰ *importance* significance
²² *happily* haply, perhaps

of wonder is broken out within this hour that ballad-
makers cannot be able to express it.

Enter another Gentleman.

Here comes the Lady Paulina's steward; he can
deliver you more. How goes it now, sir? This news,
30 which is called true, is so like an old tale that the
verity of it is in strong suspicion. Has the King
found his heir?

Third Gentleman. Most true, if ever truth were pregnant by circumstance;° that which you hear you'll
35 swear you see, there is such unity in the proofs. The
mantle of Queen Hermione; her jewel about the
neck of it; the letters of Antigonus found with it,
which they know to be his character;° the majesty
of the creature, in resemblance of the mother; the
40 affection° of nobleness, which nature shows above
her breeding and many other evidences—proclaim
her, with all certainty, to be the King's daughter.
Did you see the meeting of the two kings?

Second Gentleman. No.

45 *Third Gentleman.* Then have you lost a sight which
was to be seen, cannot be spoken of. There might
you have beheld one joy crown another, so and in
such manner that it seemed Sorrow wept to take
leave of them; for their joy waded in tears. There
50 was casting up of eyes, holding up of hands, with
countenance° of such distraction that they were to
be known by garment, not by favor.° Our king,
being ready to leap out of himself for joy of his
found daughter, as if that joy were now become a
55 loss, cries, "Oh, thy mother, thy mother"; then asks
Bohemia forgiveness, then embraces his son-in-law;
then again worries he his daughter with clipping°
her. Now he thanks the old shepherd, which stands

33–34 *truth . . . circumstance* made evident by, filled out by circumstances 38 *character* handwriting 40 *affection* natural disposition
51 *countenance* (probably meant as a plural; a common orthographical
feature in Shakespearean texts) 52 *favor* features 57 *clipping* embracing

by, like a weather-bitten conduit° of many kings'
reigns. I never heard of such another encounter,   60
which lames report to follow it, and undoes description to do it.°

Second Gentleman. What, pray you, became of Antigonus, that carried hence the child?

Third Gentleman. Like an old tale still, which will   65
have matter to rehearse, though credit° be asleep,
and not an ear open: he was torn to pieces with°
a bear. This avouches the shepherd's son, who has
not only his innocence° (which seems much) to
justify him, but a handkerchief and rings of his   70
that Paulina knows.

First Gentleman. What became of his bark and his
followers?

Third Gentleman. Wracked the same instant of their
master's death, and in the view of the shepherd: 75
so that all the instruments which aided to expose the
child were even then lost when it was found. But
oh, the noble combat, that 'twixt joy and sorrow was
fought in Paulina! She had one eye declined for the
loss of her husband, another elevated that the oracle   80
was fulfilled. She lifted the Princess from the earth,
and so locks her in embracing as if she would pin
her to her heart, that she might no more be in danger
of losing.°

First Gentleman. The dignity of this act was worth   85
the audience of kings and princes, for by such was
it acted.

Third Gentleman. One of the prettiest touches of all,
and that which angled for mine eyes—caught the
water though not the fish—was, when at the rela-   90
tion of the Queen's death, with the manner how she
came to 't bravely confessed and lamented by the
King, how attentiveness wounded his daughter; till,

---

⁵⁹ *weather-bitten conduit* weather-worn fountain (the old man's tears
make him resemble a fountain in human shape)   ⁶² *do it* describe it
⁶⁶ *credit* belief   ⁶⁷ *with* by   ⁶⁹ *innocence* simplicity   ⁸⁴ *losing* being
lost

from one sign of dolor to another, she did, with an
95 "Alas"—I would fain say—bleed tears; for I am
sure my heart wept blood. Who was most marble
there changed color; some swooned, all sorrowed.
If all the world could have seen 't, the woe had been
universal.

100 *First Gentleman.* Are they returned to the court?

Third Gentleman. No, the Princess, hearing of her
mother's statue, which is in the keeping of Paulina—
a piece many years in doing and now newly per-
formed° by that rare Italian master, Julio Ro-
105 mano,° who, had he himself eternity and could put
breath into his work, would beguile Nature of her
custom, so perfectly he is her ape:° he so near to
Hermione hath done Hermione, that they say one
would speak to her and stand in hope of answer.
110 Thither with all greediness of affection are they
gone, and there they intend to sup.

Second Gentleman. I thought she had some great matter there in hand, for she hath privately, twice or
thrice a day, ever since the death of Hermione,
115 visited that removed house. Shall we thither, and
with our company piece° the rejoicing?

First Gentleman. Who would be thence that has the
benefit of access? Every wink of an eye some new
grace will be born. Our absence makes us un-
120 thrifty to our knowledge.° Let's along.

                    Exit [with the other Gentlemen].

Autolycus. Now, had I not the dash of my former life
in me, would preferment drop on my head. I

---

¹⁰³⁻⁰⁴ *performed* completed   ¹⁰⁴⁻⁰⁵ *Julio Romano* (Italian painter
[1492–1546]. This allusion has caused much debate, because of the
anachronism, and because Julio is remembered not as a sculptor but
as a painter, though he probably practiced sculpture as well)
¹⁰⁵⁻⁰⁷ *had he himself . . . ape* had he this other attribute of God and
could put breath into his statues, he would cheat Nature of her trade,
so closely can he imitate her (the sentiment is a little confused)
¹¹⁶ *piece* i.e., add to   ¹¹⁹⁻²⁰ *unthrifty to our knowledge* careless in
the accumulation of knowledge

brought the old man and his son aboard the Prince;
told him I heard them talk of a fardel and I know
not what; but he at that time overfond of the shep-   *125*
herd's daughter (so he then took her to be), who
began to be much seasick, and himself little better,
extremity of weather continuing, this mystery remained undiscovered. But 'tis all one to me; for had
I been the finder-out of this secret, it would not have   *130*
relished° among my other discredits.

Enter Shepherd and Clown.

Here come those I have done good to against my
will, and already appearing in the blossoms of their
fortune.

Shepherd. Come, boy, I am past moe children; but thy   *135*
sons and daughters will be all gentlemen born.

Clown. You are well met, sir. You denied to fight with
me this other day, because I was no gentleman
born. See you these clothes? Say you see them not
and think me still no gentleman born; you were   *140*
best say these robes are not gentlemen born. Give
me the lie, do; and try whether I am not now a
gentleman born.

Autolycus. I know you are now, sir, a gentleman born.

Clown. Ay, and have been so any time these four   *145*
hours.

Shepherd. And so have I, boy.

Clown. So you have; but I was a gentleman born before my father; for the King's son took me by the
hand and called me brother; and then the two   *150*
kings called my father brother; and then the Prince,
(my brother) and the Princess (my sister) called
my father father; and so we wept; and there was
the first gentlemanlike tears that ever we shed.

Shepherd. We may live, son, to shed many more.   *155*

---

¹³¹ *relished* proved tasteful, acceptable

Clown. Ay; or else 'twere hard luck, being in so pre-
posterous° estate as we are.

Autolycus. I humbly beseech you, sir, to pardon me
all the faults I have committed to your worship, and
160   to give me your good report to the Prince, my master.

Shepherd. Prithee, son, do: for we must be gentle,
now we are gentlemen.

Clown. Thou wilt amend thy life?

165 *Autolycus.* Ay, an it like° your good worship.

Clown. Give me thy hand. I will swear to the Prince
thou art as honest a true° fellow as any is in Bohemia.

Shepherd. You may say it, but not swear it.

170 *Clown.* Not swear it, now I am a gentleman? Let
boors and franklins° say it, I'll swear it.

Shepherd. How if it be false, son?

Clown. If it be ne'er so false, a true gentleman may
swear it in the behalf of his friend; and I'll swear
175   to the Prince thou art a tall fellow of thy hands,°
and that thou wilt not be drunk; but I know thou
art no tall fellow of thy hands, and that thou wilt
be drunk; but I'll swear it, and I would thou
wouldst be a tall fellow of thy hands.

180 *Autolycus.* I will prove so, sir, to my power.°

Clown. Ay, by any means prove a tall fellow. If I do
not wonder how thou dar'st venture to be drunk, not
being a tall fellow, trust me not. Hark, the kings
and the princes, our kindred, are going to see the
185   Queen's picture. Come, follow us; we'll be thy good
masters.   *Exeunt.*

156–57 *preposterous* (malapropism for "prosperous")   165 *an it like* if
it please   167 *true* honest (as opposed to thieving)   171 *boors and
franklins* peasants and yeomen   175 *a tall fellow of thy hands* a man of
courage   180 *to my power* as far as I am able

Scene III. [*Sicilia, a chapel in Paulina's house.*]

Enter Leontes, Polixenes, Florizel, Perdita, Camillo,
            Paulina, Lords, etc.

Leontes. O grave and good Paulina, the great comfort
  That I have had of thee!

Paulina.   What, sovereign sir,
  I did not well, I meant well. All my services
  You have paid home.° But that you have vouch-
      safed,
  With your crowned brother and these your con-
      tracted°   5
  Heirs of your kingdoms, my poor house to visit,
  It is a surplus of your grace, which never
  My life may last to answer.

Leontes.   O Paulina,
  We honor you with trouble; but we came
  To see the statue of our queen. Your gallery   10
  Have we passed through, not without much content
  In many singularities;° but we saw not
  That which my daughter came to look upon,
  The statue of her mother.

Paulina.   As she lived peerless,
  So her dead likeness I do well believe   15
  Excels whatever yet you looked upon,
  Or hand of man hath done; therefore I keep it
  Lonely, apart. But here it is; prepare
  To see the life as lively mocked, as ever
  Still sleep mocked death: behold, and say 'tis well.   20

V.iii.⁴ *paid home* paid in full   ⁵ *your contracted* (this "your" should
possibly be omitted; the compositor could have caught it from "your
crowned" or from the next line)   ¹² *singularities* varieties

[Paulina draws a curtain and discovers] Hermione
[standing] like a statue.

I like your silence; it the more shows off
Your wonder; but yet speak, first you, my liege.
Comes it not something near?

Leontes.   Her natural posture!
Chide me, dear stone, that I may say indeed
25 Thou art Hermione; or rather, thou art she
In thy not chiding; for she was as tender
As infancy and grace. But yet, Paulina,
Hermione was not so much wrinkled, nothing
So agèd as this seems.

Polixenes.   Oh, not by much.

30 *Paulina.* So much the more our carver's excellence,
Which lets go by some sixteen years, and makes her
As she lived° now.

Leontes.   As now she might have done,
So much to my good comfort, as it is
Now piercing to my soul. Oh, thus she stood,
35 Even with such life of majesty—warm life,
As now it coldly stands—when first I wooed her.
I am ashamed: does not the stone rebuke me,
For being more stone than it? O royal piece!
There's magic in thy majesty, which has
40 My evils conjured to remembrance,° and
From thy admiring daughter took the spirits,
Standing like stone with thee.

Perdita.   And give me leave,
And do not say 'tis superstition that
I kneel, and then implore her blessing. Lady,
45 Dear queen, that ended when I but began,
Give me that hand of yours to kiss.

Paulina.   O, patience!
The statue is but newly fixed, the color's
Not dry.

32 *As she lived* as if she lived   39–40 *magic . . . conjured . . . remem-*
brance (the sight of the statue has called up his sins into his mind as
a magician summons demons)

Camillo. My lord, your sorrow was too sore laid on,
　　Which sixteen winters cannot blow away,   50
　　So many summers dry. Scarce any joy
　　Did ever so long live; no sorrow
　　But killed itself much sooner.

Polixenes.   Dear my brother,
　　Let him that was the cause of this have power
　　To take off so much grief from you as he   55
　　Will piece up° in himself.

Paulina.   Indeed, my lord,
　　If I had thought the sight of my poor image
　　Would thus have wrought you—for the stone is mine—
　　I'd not have showed it.

Leontes.   Do not draw the curtain.

Paulina. No longer shall you gaze on 't, lest your fancy   60
　　May think anon it moves.

Leontes.   Let be, let be!
　　Would I were dead, but that methinks already°—
　　What was he that did make it? See, my lord,
　　Would you not deem it breathed? And that those veins
　　Did verily bear blood?

Polixenes.   Masterly done!   65
　　The very life seems warm upon her lip.

Leontes. The fixure° of her eye has motion in 't,
　　As we are mocked with art.

Paulina.   I'll draw the curtain;
　　My lord's almost so far transported that
　　He'll think anon it lives.

Leontes.   O sweet Paulina,   70
　　Make me to think so twenty years together!
　　No settled° senses of the world can match
　　The pleasure of that madness. Let 't alone.

―――――――――――――――――――――――――――――――
56 *piece up* make his own   **62** *Would . . . already* May I die if I do
not think it moves already (Staunton)   **67** *fixure* (early form of "fix-
ture")   **72** *settled* sane

Paulina. I am sorry, sir, I have thus far stirred you;
  but
    I could afflict you farther.

75 *Leontes.*   Do, Paulina;
      For this affliction has a taste as sweet
      As any cordial° comfort. Still, methinks,
      There is an air comes from her. What fine chisel
      Could ever yet cut breath? Let no man mock me,
      For I will kiss her.

80 *Paulina.*   Good my lord, forbear!
      The ruddiness upon her lip is wet;
      You'll mar it if you kiss it; stain your own
      With oily painting. Shall I draw the curtain?

Leontes. No, not these twenty years.

Perdita.   So long could I
      Stand by, a looker-on.

85 *Paulina.*   Either forbear,
      Quit presently the chapel, or resolve you
      For more amazement. If you can behold it,
      I'll make the statue move indeed, descend,
      And take you by the hand—but then you'll think,
90   Which I protest against, I am assisted
      By wicked powers.

Leontes.   What you can make her do,
      I am content to look on; what to speak,
      I am content to hear; for 'tis as easy
      To make her speak, as move.

Paulina.   It is required
95   You do awake your faith; then, all stand still.
      Or those that think it is unlawful business
      I am about, let them depart.

Leontes.   Proceed.
      No foot shall stir.

Paulina.   Music, awake her: strike.
      'Tis time; descend; be stone no more; approach;

----

77 *cordial* heart-warming

Strike all that look upon with marvel; come;   100
I'll fill your grave up. Stir; nay, come away;
Bequeath to death your numbness, for from him
Dear life redeems you. You perceive she stirs.

[*Hermione comes down.*]

Start not; her actions shall be holy as
You hear my spell is lawful. Do not shun her   105
Until you see her die again, for then
You kill her double. Nay, present your hand.
When she was young, you wooed her; now, in age,
Is she become the suitor?

Leontes.   Oh, she's warm!
If this be magic, let it be an art   110
Lawful as eating.

Polixenes.   She embraces him.

Camillo. She hangs about his neck;
If she pertain to life, let her speak too.

Polixenes. Ay, and make it manifest where she has
    lived,
Or how stol'n from the dead.

Paulina.   That she is living,   115
Were it but told you, should be hooted at
Like an old tale; but it appears she lives,
Though yet she speak not. Mark a little while:
Please you to interpose, fair madam; kneel,
And pray your mother's blessing; turn, good lady,   120
Our Perdita is found.

Hermione.   You gods look down,
And from your sacred vials pour your graces
Upon my daughter's head! Tell me, mine own,
Where hast thou been preserved? Where lived? How
    found
Thy father's court? For thou shalt hear that I,   125
Knowing by Paulina that the oracle
Gave hope thou wast in being,° have preserved
Myself to see the issue.

¹²⁷ *in being* alive

Paulina.   There's time enough for that,
Lest they desire upon this push° to trouble
130   Your joys with like relation. Go together,
You precious winners all; your exultation
Partake° to every one. I an old turtle,
Will wing me to some withered bough, and there
My mate, that's never to be found again,
Lament till I am lost.

135 *Leontes.*   O peace, Paulina!
Thou shouldst a husband take by my consent,
As I by thine a wife. This is a match,
And made between 's by vows. Thou hast found
    mine,
But how, is to be questioned; for I saw her,
140   As I thought, dead; and have in vain said many
A prayer upon her grave. I'll not seek farre,°
For him, I partly know his mind, to find thee
An honorable husband. Come, Camillo,
And take her by the hand, whose worth and
    honesty°
145 Is richly noted, and here justified
By us, a pair of kings. Let's from this place.
What! Look upon my brother.° Both your pardons,
That e'er I put between your holy looks
My ill suspicion. This your son-in-law,
150   And son unto the King, whom, heavens directing,
Is troth-plight to your daughter. Good Paulina,
Lead us from hence, where we may leisurely
Each one demand and answer to his part
Performed in this wide gap of time since first
155   We were dissevered. Hastily lead away.   *Exeunt.*

FINIS

---

129 *upon this push* at this exciting moment   132 *Partake* communicate,
share   141 *farre* farther   144 *whose worth and honesty* i.e., Camillo's
147 *Look upon my brother* (Hermione has presumably shown some
natural embarrassment about greeting Polixenes)

Textual Note

The Winter's Tale was placed at the end of the section of Comedies in the Folio of 1623. There was no earlier edition, and so all subsequent editions derive from the Folio text. Bibliographical evidence shows that the play was added to the Folio late, when a number of the History plays had already been printed. Possibly no copy was available until then. The copy that eventually reached the printing house was almost certainly a transcript of the play made by Ralph Crane, whose hand is now well known to scholars. Crane did a good deal for Shakespeare's company, the King's Men, and the Folio texts of *The Tempest, The Two Gentlemen of Verona*— and possibly other plays too—are attributable to him. Certain of his characteristics—notably his fondness for brackets and his habit of placing all the entries at the head of the scene, whether or no they are repeated when the character actually comes in—are abundantly in evidence in the Folio text of *The Winter's Tale*.

The text is very deficient in stage directions, and Crane's copy was evidently not made for use in the playhouse. But he was an intelligent scribe, and doubtless gave the compositor clean copy. In fact, this is one of the cleanest of Shakespeare's texts, despite the difficulty of some of the verse. The present edition deletes the superfluous entries at heads of scenes and places them at the appropriate positions, modernizes spelling and punctuation, and translates from Latin into English the Folio's act and

scene divisions. The list of characters, here prefixed to
the play, in the Folio follows the play. Other material
departures from the Folio text are listed below in italic type,
followed by the Folio's reading (F) in roman; only in three
or four places is there any real difficulty involved.

I.i.28 *have* hath

I.ii.104 *And* A   158 *do* does   208 *you, they say* you say
276 *hobby-horse* Holy-horse   327–28 *sully/The purity* Sully the
puritie   446–47 *thereon,/ His execution sworn* Thereon his Execution sworne

II.i.25–26 *I have one/Of* I have one of

II.ii.6 *whom* who   52 *let't* le't

II.iii.38 *What* Who   52 *profess* professes   176 *its* it

III.ii.1 *session* Sessions   10 *Silence* [F italicizes, as if s.d.]   32 *Who*
Whom   107 *for* no

III.iii.18 *awaking* a waking   119 *made* mad

IV.iii.10 *with heigh, with heigh* With heigh   57 *offends* offend

IV.iv.2 *do* Do's   12 *Digest it with* Digest with   13 *swoon* sworne
98 *your* you   160 *out* on't   365 *who* whom   423 *acknowledged*
acknowledge   427 *who* whom   432 *shalt see* shalt neuer see
443 *hoop* hope   471 *your* my   494 *hide* hides   503 *whom* who
553 *asks thee, the son, forgiveness* asks thee there Sonne forgiue-
nesse   709 *know not* know   739 *or toaze* at toaze   849 *Exit*
Exeunt

V.i.12 *True, too true* [F places the first "true" at the end of
Leontes' previous speech]   61 *just cause* just such cause   75 *I have
done* [F gives to Cleomenes]

V.ii.36 *Hermione* Hermiones

V.iii.18 *Lonely* Louely   96 *Or* on

The Source of *The Winter's Tale*

Shakespeare's source was a *novella* by his old enemy Robert Greene. The title of the first edition reads:

Pandosto. The Triumph of Time. Wherein is discouered by a pleasant Historie, that although by the meanes of sinister fortune, Truth may be concealed, yet by Time in spight of fortune it is most manifestly reuealed. Pleasant for age to auoyde drowsie thoughtes, profitable for youth to eschue other wanton pastimes, and bringing to both a desired content. *Temporis filia veritas*. By Robert Greene, Maister of Artes in Cambridge. *Omne tulit punctum qui miscuit vtile dulci*. Imprinted at London by Thomas Orwin for Thomas Cadman, dwelling at the Signe of the Bible, neere vnto the North doore of Paules, 1588.

The Short Title Catalogue records only one copy of this edition, in the British Museum; and that is imperfect. There were subsequent editions in 1592, 1595, 1607, and later. But although there was so recent an edition available, Shakespeare appears to have used the first. He seems for some reason to have been interested in Greene at this time, for he also drew on the pamphleteer's popular studies of the London underworld, especially *The Second Part of Conny-catching* (1591), useful for describing the tricks of Autolycus (especially the cheating of the Clown in IV.iii); and although he rejected Greene's personal names, he replaced "Garinter" by "Mamillius," perhaps remembering Greene's "looking glass for the ladies of England," *Mamillia* (1583).

Shakespeare treats *Pandosto* in his usual way, freely changing it but often echoing its language and incidents. The following very brief summary uses the names Shakespeare gave the characters.

Shakespeare changes the countries about; Leontes is king of Bohemia, Polixenes of Sicily; and it is the wife of Polixenes who is daughter of the empress of Russia, not Hermione. Greene's Hermione, though perfectly innocent, gives more color to the suspicions of Leontes by the freedom of her conduct toward Polixenes. She does not discover her pregnancy till she is already in prison. Camillo shows more self-interest in the novel, and has no part in the return of Perdita to her father. The jealousy of Leontes, though not well founded, is less of a brainstorm in the original. He sends the new baby to sea in a little boat by herself; there is no Antigonus. After the trial he instantly accepts the word of the oracle, but his son and his wife both die. Perdita is cast ashore in Sicily and reared by shepherds interested in the gold that accompanies her. Years later, she is wooed by Florizel, but here the tone of the novel is very different from that of the play, despite suggestions that Shakespeare used in the sheep-shearing scene. Florizel is much more formal, and the relationship, until Perdita, properly suspicious, alters it by insisting on her virtue, is not much different from an ordinary seduction of a country girl by a courtier. But Florizel, appearing as a shepherd, establishes the honesty of his intentions and plans to amass money to elope with Perdita to Italy. The unhappy old shepherd is tricked into boarding the ship (but not by Autolycus, who does not exist in the novel). When the couple arrives in Bohemia, Leontes conceives a lustful desire for Perdita, and throws Florizel into prison. But when he hears the whole story from the ambassadors of Polixenes (who is alarmed to think of his son in the hands of an enemy), he frees Florizel and condemns Perdita and her father to death. But the old man now tells his tale; Perdita is proved

to be Leontes' lost daughter. She returns to Sicily with
Florizel, and they are married; but Leontes kills himself
from remorse.

I have given no account of many changes that are simply
a matter of dramaturgical economy. Despite the strong
similarities in plot, there are important alterations in
Shakespeare. The greatest of these, if the least tangible, is
his substitution of Nature for Fortune as the deity presiding over the original story; and the consequent reconstruc-
tion in the statue scene, with Hermione restored and
Leontes transported with joy at the recovery of his wife,
his daughter, and his friend. For Shakespeare's Perdita and
Florizel, Greene affords little more than hints, and the
whole pastoral of the Fourth Act is similarly built on mere
suggestions. Greene's Florizel knows better than to speak
freely of his love; and Polixenes does not visit the sheep-
fold, let alone converse with Perdita on profound topics.
The point at which the two works most closely concur is
the scene of Hermione's trial, though the reader will see
that other references to Greene's text are fairly frequent,
so that it looks as if Shakespeare had the book on his
desk. It was the story he wanted, to adapt as freely as he
chose, and he shuns the Arcadianism of Greene's dialogue;
yet once again the dead author might have found cause to
complain, as he had eighteen years earlier, that the upstart
"crow" had been "beautified with our feathers."

Selections from Robert Greene: *Pandosto*

Among all the passions wherewith human minds are
perplexed, there is none that so galleth with restless despite
as the infectious sore of jealousy; for all other griefs are
either to be appeased with sensible persuasions, to be
cured with wholesome counsel, to be relieved in want, or

by tract of time to be worn out, jealousy only excepted, which is so sauced with suspicious doubts and pinching mistrust, that whoso seeks by friendly counsel to raze out this hellish passion, it forthwith suspecteth that he giveth this advice to cover his own guiltiness. Yea, whoso is pained with this restless torment doubteth all, distrusteth himself, is always frozen with fear and fired with suspicion, having that wherein consisteth all his joy to be the breeder of his misery. Yea, it is such a heavy enemy to that holy estate of matrimony, sowing between the married couples such deadly seeds of secret hatred, as, love being once razed out by spiteful distrust, there oft ensueth bloody revenge, as this ensuing history manifestly proveth: wherein Pandosto, furiously incensed by causeless jealousy, procured the death of his most loving and loyal wife and his own endless sorrow and misery.

In the country of Bohemia, there reigned a king called Pandosto, whose fortunate success in wars against his foes, and bountiful courtesy toward his friends in peace, made him to be greatly feared and loved of all men. This Pandosto had to wife a lady called Bellaria, by birth royal, learned by education, fair by nature, by virtues famous, so that it was hard to judge whether her beauty, fortune, or virtue won the greatest commendations. These two, linked together in perfect love, led their lives with such fortunate content that their subjects greatly rejoiced to see their quiet disposition. They had not been married long, but Fortune, willing to increase their happiness, lent them a son, so adorned with the gifts of nature, as the perfection of the child greatly augmented the love of the parents and the joy of their commons. . . .

Fortune, envious of such happy success, willing to show some sign of her inconstancy, turned her wheel, and darkened their bright sun of prosperity with the misty clouds of mishap and misery. For it so happened that Egistus, king of Sicilia, who in his youth had been brought up with Pandosto, desirous to show that neither tract of time nor distance of place could diminish their former friendship, provided a navy of ships and sailed into

Bohemia to visit his old friend and companion; who, hearing of his arrival, went himself in person and his wife Bellaria, accompanied with a great train of lords and ladies, to meet Egistus; and espying him, alighted from his horse, embraced him very lovingly, protesting that nothing in the world could have happened more acceptable to him than his coming, wishing his wife to welcome his old friend and acquaintance: who, to show how she liked him whom her husband loved, entertained him with such familiar courtesy as Egistus perceived himself to be very well welcome. . . .

Bellaria, who in her time was the flower of courtesy, willing to show how unfeignedly she loved her husband by his friend's entertainment, used him likewise so familiarly that her countenance bewrayed how her mind was affected towards him, oftentimes coming herself into his bed-chamber to see that nothing should be amiss to mislike him. This honest familiarity increased daily more and more betwixt them; for Bellaria, noting in Egistus a princely and bountiful mind, adorned with sundry and excellent qualities, and Egistus, finding in her a virtuous and courteous disposition, there grew such a secret uniting of their affections, that the one could not well be without the company of the other: insomuch, that when Pandosto was busied with such urgent affairs that he could not be present with his friend Egistus, Bellaria would walk with him into the garden, where they two in private and pleasant devices would pass away the time to both their contents. This custom still continuing betwixt them, a certain melancholy passion entering the mind of Pandosto drave him into sundry and doubtful thoughts. First, he called to mind the beauty of his wife Bellaria, the comeliness and bravery of his friend Egistus, thinking that love was above all laws and, therefore, to be stayed with no law; that it was hard to put fire and flax together without burning; that their open pleasures might breed his secret displeasures. He considered with himself that Egistus was a man and must needs love, that his wife was a woman, and therefore, subject unto love, and that where fancy forced, friendship was of no force.

These and suchlike doubtful thoughts, a long time smothering in his stomach, began at last to kindle in his mind a secret mistrust, which, increased by suspicion, grew at last to a flaming jealousy that so tormented him as he could take no rest. He then began to measure all their actions, and to misconstrue of their too private familiarity, judging that it was not for honest affection, but for disordinate fancy, so that he began to watch them more narrowly to see if he could get any true or certain proof to confirm his doubtful suspicion. While thus he noted their looks and gestures and suspected their thoughts and meanings, they two silly souls, who doubted nothing of this his treacherous intent, frequented daily each other's company, which drave him into such a frantic passion, that he began to bear a secret hate to Egistus and a louring countenance to Bellaria; who marveling at such unaccustomed frowns, began to cast beyond the moon, and to enter into a thousand sundry thoughts, which way she should offend her husband: but finding in herself a clear conscience ceased to muse, until such time as she might find fit opportunity to demand the cause of his dumps. In the meantime Pandosto's mind was so far charged with jealousy, that he did no longer doubt, but was assured, as he thought, that his friend Egistus had entered a wrong point in his tables, and so had played him false play: whereupon, desirous to revenge so great an injury, he thought best to dissemble the grudge with a fair and friendly countenance, and so under the shape of a friend to show him the trick of a foe. Devising with himself a long time how he might best put away Egistus without suspicion of treacherous murder, he concluded at last to poison him; which opinion pleasing his humor he became resolute in his determination, and the better to bring the matter to pass he called unto him his cupbearer, with whom in secret he brake the matter, promising to him for the performance thereof to give him a thousand crowns of yearly revenues.

His cupbearer, either being of a good conscience or willing for fashion sake to deny such a bloody request, began with great reasons to persuade Pandosto from his determin-

ate mischief, showing him what an offense murder was to the
gods; how such unnatural actions did more displease the
heavens than men, that causeless cruelty did seldom or
never escape without revenge: he laid before his face
that Egistus was his friend, a king, and one that was come
into his kingdom to confirm a league of perpetual amity
betwixt them; that he had and did show him a most
friendly countenance; how Egistus was not only honored
of his own people by obedience, but also loved of the
Bohemians for his courtesy, and that if he now should
without any just or manifest cause poison him, it would
not only be a great dishonor to his majesty, and a means
to sow perpetual enmity between the Sicilians and the
Bohemians, but also his own subjects would repine at
such treacherous cruelty. These and suchlike persuasions
of Franion—for so was his cupbearer called—could no
whit prevail to dissuade him from his devilish enterprise,
but, remaining resolute in his determination (his fury
so fired with rage as it could not be appeased with reason),
he began with bitter taunts to take up his man, and to
lay before him two baits, preferment and death; saying
that if he should poison Egistus, he would advance him
to high dignities; if he refused to do it of an obstinate mind,
no torture should be too great to requite his disobedience.
Franion, seeing that to persuade Pandosto any more was
but to strive against the stream, consented, as soon as
opportunity would give him leave, to dispatch Egistus:
wherewith Pandosto remained somewhat satisfied, hoping
now he should be fully revenged of such mistrusted injuries, intending also as soon as Egistus was dead to give
his wife a sop of the same sauce, and so be rid of those
which were the cause of his restless sorrow. . . .

. . . Franion . . . seeing either he must die with a
clear mind, or live with a spotted conscience, he was so
cumbered with divers cogitations that he could take no
rest, until at last he determined to break the matter to
Egistus; but, fearing that the king should either suspect
or hear of such matters, he concealed the device till opportunity would permit him to reveal it. Lingering thus
in doubtful fear, in an evening he went to Egistus' lodging,

and desirous to break with him of certain affairs that
touched the king, after all were commanded out of the
chamber, Franion made manifest the whole conspiracy
which Pandosto had devised against him, desiring Egistus
not to account him a traitor for bewraying his master's
counsel, but to think that he did it for conscience: hoping
that although his master, inflamed with rage or incensed
by some sinister reports or slanderous speeches, had
imagined such causeless mischief, yet when time should
pacify his anger, and try those talebearers but flattering
parasites, then he would count him as a faithful servant
that with such care had kept his master's credit. Egistus
had not fully heard Franion tell forth his tale, but a
quaking fear possessed all his limbs, thinking that there
was some treason wrought, and that Franion did but
shadow his craft with these false colors: wherefore he
began to wax in choler, and said that he doubted not
Pandosto, sith he was his friend, and there had never
as yet been any breach of amity. He had not sought to
invade his lands, to conspire with his enemies, to dissuade his subjects from their allegiance; but in word and
thought he rested his at all times: he knew not, therefore,
any cause that should move Pandosto to seek his death,
but suspected it to be a compacted knavery of the Bohemians to bring the king and him at odds.

Franion, staying him in the midst of his talk, told him
that to dally with princes was with the swans to sing against
their death, and that, if the Bohemians had intended any
such mischief, it might have been better brought to pass
than by revealing the conspiracy: therefore his majesty
did ill to misconstrue of his good meaning, sith his intent
was to hinder treason, not to become a traitor; and to
confirm his promises, if it pleased his majesty to fly into
Sicilia for the safeguard of his life, he would go with him,
and if then he found not such a practice to be pretended,
let his imagined treachery be repaid with most monstrous
torments. Egistus, hearing the solemn protestation of Franion, began to consider that in love and kingdoms neither
faith nor law is to be respected, doubting that Pandosto
thought by his death to destroy his men, and with speedy

war to invade Sicilia. These and such doubts throughly weighed, he gave great thanks to Franion, promising if he might with life return to Syracusa, that he would create him a duke in Sicilia, craving his counsel how he might escape out of the country. . . .

. . . Egistus, fearing that delay might breed danger, and willing that the grass should not be cut from under his feet, taking bag and baggage, by the help of Franion conveyed himself and his men out at a postern gate of the city, so secretly and speedily that without any suspicion they got to the seashore; where, with many a bitter curse taking their leave of Bohemia, they went aboard. Weighing their anchors and hoisting sail, they passed as fast as wind and sea would permit towards Sicilia, Egistus being a joyful man that he had safely passed such treacherous perils. But as they were quietly floating on the sea, so Pandosto and his citizens were in an uproar; for, seeing that the Sicilians without taking their leave were fled away by night, the Bohemians feared some treason, and the king thought that without question his suspicion was true, seeing his cupbearer had bewrayed the sum of his secret pretense. Whereupon he began to imagine that Franion and his wife Bellaria had conspired with Egistus, and that the fervent affection she bare him was the only means of his secret departure; insomuch that, incensed with rage, he commands that his wife should be carried to strait prison until they heard further of his pleasure. The guard, unwilling to lay their hands on such a virtuous princess and yet fearing the king's fury, went very sorrowful to fulfill their charge. Coming to the queen's lodging they found her playing with her young son Garinter, unto whom with tears doing the message, Bellaria, astonished at such a hard censure and finding her clear conscience a sure advocate to plead in her case, went to the prison most willingly, where with sighs and tears she passed away the time till she might come to her trial.

But Pandosto, whose reason was suppressed with rage and whose unbridled folly was incensed with fury, seeing Franion had bewrayed his secrets, and that Egistus might well be railed on, but not revenged, determined to wreak all his wrath on poor Bellaria. He, therefore, caused a general proclamation to be made through all his realm that the queen and Egistus had, by the help of Franion, not only committed most incestuous adultery, but also had conspired the king's death; whereupon the traitor Franion was fled away with Egistus, and Bellaria was most justly imprisoned. This proclamation being once blazed through the country, although the virtuous disposition of the queen did half discredit the contents, yet the sudden and speedy passage of Egistus and the secret departure of Franion induced them, the circumstances throughly considered, to think that both the proclamation was true, and the king greatly injured: yet they pitied her case, as sorrowful that so good a lady should be crossed with such adverse fortune. But the king, whose restless rage would admit no pity, thought that although he might sufficiently requite his wife's falsehood with the bitter plague of pinching penury, yet his mind should never be glutted with revenge till he might have fit time and opportunity to repay the treachery of Egistus with a fatal injury. But a curst cow hath ofttimes short horns, and a willing mind but a weak arm; for Pandosto, although he felt that revenge was a spur to war, and that envy always proffereth steel, yet he saw that Egistus was not only of great puissance and prowess to withstand him, but had also many kings of his alliance to aid him, if need should serve, for he married the emperor's daughter of Russia. These and the like considerations something daunted Pandosto his courage, so that he was content rather to put up a manifest injury with peace, than hunt after revenge, dishonor, and loss; determining, since Egistus had escaped scot-free, that Bellaria should pay for all at an unreasonable price.

Remaining thus resolute in his determination, Bellaria continuing still in prison and hearing the contents of the proclamation, knowing that her mind was never touched with such affection, nor that Egistus had ever offered her such discourtesy, would gladly have come to her answer, that both she might have known her just accusers, and cleared herself of that guiltless crime.

But Pandosto was so inflamed with rage and infected

with jealousy, as he would not vouchsafe to hear her, nor admit any just excuse; so that she was fain to make a virtue of her need and with patience to bear those heavy injuries. As thus she lay crossed with calamities, a great cause to increase her grief, she found herself quick with child. . . .

. . . The jailer, pitying those her heavy passions, thinking that if the king knew she were with child he would somewhat appease his fury and release her from prison, went in all haste and certified Pandosto what the effect of Bellaria's complaint was; who no sooner heard the jailer say she was with child, but as one possessed with a frenzy he rose up in a rage, swearing that she and the bastard brat she was big withal should die if the gods themselves said no; thinking that surely by computation of time that Egistus and not he was the father to the child. This suspicious thought galled afresh this half-healed sore, insomuch as he could take no rest until he might mitigate his choler with a just revenge, which happened presently after. For Bellaria was brought to bed of a fair and beautiful daughter, which no sooner Pandosto heard, but he determined that both Bellaria and the young infant should be burnt with fire. His nobles hearing of the king's cruel sentence sought by persuasions to divert him from his bloody determination, laying before his face the innocency of the child, and virtuous disposition of his wife, how she had continually loved and honored him so tenderly that without due proof he could not, nor ought not, to appeach her of that crime. And if she had faulted, yet it were more honorable to pardon with mercy than to punish with extremity, and more kingly to be commended of pity than accused of rigor. And as for the child, if he should punish it for the mother's offense, it were to strive against nature and justice; and that unnatural actions do more offend the gods than men; how causeless cruelty nor innocent blood never scapes without revenge. These and suchlike reasons could not appease his rage, but he rested resolute in this, that Bellaria being an adultress the child was a bastard, and he would not suffer that such an infamous brat should call him father. Yet at last, seeing his

noblemen were importunate upon him, he was content to
spare the child's life, and yet to put it to a worse death.
For he found out this device, that seeing, as he thought,
it came by fortune, so he would commit it to the charge
of fortune; and, therefore, he caused a little cockboat to
be provided, wherein he meant to put the babe, and then
send it to the mercies of the seas and the destinies. From
this his peers in no wise could persuade him, but that he
sent presently two of his guard to fetch the child. . . .

[Bellaria, hearing of her husband's intention, first faints,
and then laments the fate of her child.] . . . Such and so
great was her grief, that her vital spirits being suppressed
with sorrow, she fell again down into a trance, having her
senses so sotted with care that after she was revived yet
she lost her memory, and lay for a great time without
moving, as one in a trance. The guard left her in this
perplexity, and carried the child to the king, who, quite
devoid of pity, commanded that without delay it should
be put in the boat, having neither sail nor rudder to guide
it, and so to be carried into the midst of the sea, and there
left to the wind and wave as the destinies please to
appoint. . . .

[The child is taken away by sailors and put to sea in a
storm.]

. . . But leaving the child to her fortunes, again to
Pandosto, who not yet glutted with sufficient revenge
devised which way he should best increase his wife's
calamity. But first assembling his nobles and counselors,
he called her for the more reproach into open court, where
it was objected against her that she had committed adultery
with Egistus, and conspired with Franion to poison Pandosto her husband, but their pretense being partly spied,
she counseled them to fly away by night for their better
safety. Bellaria, who standing like a prisoner at the bar,
feeling in herself a clear conscience to withstand her false
accusers, seeing that no less than death could pacify her
husband's wrath, waxed bold and desired that she might
have law and justice, for mercy she neither craved nor
hoped for; and that those perjured wretches which had
falsely accused her to the king might be brought before her

face to give in evidence. But Pandosto, whose rage and jealousy was such as no reason nor equity could appease, told her that, for her accusers, they were of such credit as their words were sufficient witness, and that the sudden and secret flight of Egistus and Franion confirmed that which they had confessed; and as for her, it was her part to deny such a monstrous crime, and to be impudent in forswearing the fact, since she had past all shame in committing the fault: but her stale countenance should stand for no coin, for as the bastard which she bare was served, so she should with some cruel death be requited. Bellaria, no whit dismayed with this rough reply, told her husband Pandosto that he spake upon choler and not conscience, for her virtuous life had been ever such as no spot of suspicion could ever stain. And if she had borne a friendly countenance to Egistus, it was in respect he was his friend, and not for any lusting affection; therefore, if she were condemned without any further proof it was rigor and not law.

The noblemen, which sate in judgment, said that Bellaria spake reason, and entreated the king that the accusers might be openly examined and sworn, and if then the evidence were such as the jury might find her guilty (for seeing she was a prince she ought to be tried by her peers), then let her have such punishment as the extremity of the law will assign to such malefactors. The king presently made answer that in this case he might and would dispense with the law, and that the jury being once paneled they should take his word for sufficient evidence; otherwise he would make the proudest of them repent it. The noblemen seeing the king in choler were all whist; but Bellaria, whose life then hung in the balance, fearing more perpetual infamy than momentary death, told the king if his fury might stand for a law that it were vain to have the jury yield their verdict; and, therefore, she fell down upon her knees, and desired the king that for the love he bare to his young son Garinter, whom she brought into the world, that he would grant her a request; which was this, that it would please his majesty to send six of his noblemen whom he best trusted to the Isle of

Delphos, there to inquire of the oracle of Apollo whether she had committed adultery with Egistus, or conspired to poison him with Franion? and if the god Apollo, who by his divine essence knew all secrets, gave answer that she was guilty, she were content to suffer any torment were it never so terrible. The request was so reasonable that Pandosto could not for shame deny it, unless he would be counted of all his subjects more willful than wise: he therefore agreed that with as much speed as might be there should be certain ambassadors dispatched to the Isle of Delphos, and in the mean season he commanded that his wife should be kept in close prison.

[The ambassadors arrive at Delphos.] . . . They had not long kneeled at the altar, but Apollo with a loud voice said: "Bohemians, what you find behind the altar take, and depart." They forthwith obeying the oracle found a scroll of parchment, wherein was written these words in letters of gold—

THE ORACLE

SUSPICION IS NO PROOF: JEALOUSY IS AN UNEQUAL JUDGE: BELLARIA IS CHASTE: EGISTUS BLAMELESS: FRANION A TRUE SUBJECT: PANDOSTO TREACHEROUS: HIS BABE AN INNOCENT; AND THE KING SHALL LIVE WITHOUT AN HEIR, IF THAT WHICH IS LOST BE NOT FOUND.

As soon as they had taken out this scroll the priest of the god commanded them that they should not presume to read it before they came in the presence of Pandosto, unless they would incur the displeasure of Apollo. The Bohemian lords carefully obeying his command, taking their leave of the priest with great reverence, departed out of the temple, and went to their ships, and as soon as wind would permit them sailed toward Bohemia, whither in short time they safely arrived; and with great triumph issuing out of their ships went to the king's palace, whom they found in his chamber accompanied with other noblemen. Pandosto no sooner saw them but with a merry countenance he welcomed them home, asking what news? they told his majesty that they had received an answer of the god written in a scroll, but with this charge, that they should not read the contents before they came in the presence of the king, and with that they delivered him the parchment: but his noblemen entreated him that, sith therein was contained either the safety of his wife's life and honesty or her death and perpetual infamy, that he would have his nobles and commons assembled in the judgment hall, where the queen, brought in as prisoner, should hear the contents. If she were found guilty by the oracle of the god, then all should have cause to think his rigor proceeded of due desert: if her grace were found faultless, then she should be cleared before all, sith she had been accused openly. This pleased the king so, that he appointed the day, and assembled all his lords and commons, and caused the queen to be brought in before the judgment seat, commanding that the indictment should be read wherein she was accused of adultery with Egistus and of conspiracy with Franion. Bellaria hearing the contents was no whit astonished, but made this cheerful answer—

"If the divine powers be privy to human actions—as no doubt they are—I hope my patience shall make fortune blush, and my unspotted life shall stain spiteful discredit. For although lying report hath sought to appeach mine honor, and suspicion hath intended to soil my credit with infamy, yet where virtue keepeth the fort, report and suspicion may assail, but never sack: how I have led my life before Egistus' coming, I appeal, Pandosto, to the gods and to thy conscience. What hath passed betwixt him and me, the gods only know, and I hope will presently reveal: that I loved Egistus I cannot deny; that I honored him I shame not to confess: to the one I was forced by his virtues, to the other for his dignities. But as touching lascivious lust, I say Egistus is honest, and hope myself to be found without spot: for Franion, I can neither accuse him nor excuse him, for I was not privy to his departure; and that this is true which I have here rehearsed I refer myself to the divine oracle."

Bellaria had no sooner said but the king commanded that one of his dukes should read the contents of the scroll, which after the commons had heard they gave a great shout, rejoicing and clapping their hands that the queen was clear of that false accusation. But the king, whose conscience was a witness against him of his witless fury and false suspected jealousy, was so ashamed of his rash folly that he entreated his nobles to persuade Bellaria to forgive and forget these injuries; promising not only to show himself a loyal and loving husband, but also to reconcile himself to Egistus and Franion; revealing then before them all the cause of their secret flight, and how treacherously he thought to have practiced his death, if the good mind of his cupbearer had not prevented his purpose. As thus he was relating the whole matter, there was word brought him that his young son Garinter was suddenly dead, which news so soon as Bellaria heard, surcharged before with extreme joy and now suppressed with heavy sorrow, her vital spirits were so stopped that she fell down presently dead, and could be never revived. This sudden sight so appalled the king's senses, that he sank from his seat in a swound, so as he was fain to be carried by his nobles to his palace, where he lay by the space of three days without speech. His commons were, as men in despair, diversely distressed: there was nothing but mourning and lamentation to be heard throughout all Bohemia: their young prince dead, their virtuous queen bereaved of her life, and their king and sovereign in great hazard. This tragical discourse of fortune so daunted them, as they went like shadows, not men; yet somewhat to comfort their heavy hearts, they heard that Pandosto was come to himself, and had recovered his speech, who as in a fury brayed out these bitter speeches. . . .

[Pandosto reproaches himself, and is prevented from suicide. The story returns to Fawnia (Perdita).] . . .The little boat was driven with the tide into the coast of Sicilia, where sticking upon the sands it rested. Fortune minding to be wanton, willing to show that as she hath wrinkles on her brows so she hath dimples in her cheeks, thought after so many sour looks to lend a feigned smile, and after a puffing storm to bring a pretty calm, she began thus to dally. It fortuned a poor mercenary shepherd that dwelled in Sicilia, who got his living by other men's flocks, missed one of his sheep, and, thinking it had strayed into the covert that was hard by, sought very diligently to find that which he could not see, fearing either that the wolves or eagles had undone him (for he was so poor as a sheep was half his substance), wandered down toward the sea cliffs to see if perchance the sheep was browsing on the sea ivy, whereon they greatly do feed; but not finding her there, as he was ready to return to his flock he heard a child cry, but knowing there was no house near, he thought he had mistaken the sound and that it was the bleating of his sheep. Wherefore, looking more narrowly, as he cast his eye to the sea he spied a little boat, from whence, as he attentively listened, he might hear the cry to come. Standing a good while in a maze, at last he went to the shore, and wading to the boat, as he looked in he saw the little babe lying all alone ready to die for hunger and cold, wrapped in a mantle of scarlet richly embroidered with gold, and having a chain about the neck.

The shepherd, who before had never seen so fair a babe nor so rich jewels, thought assuredly that it was some little god, and began with great devotion to knock on his breast. The babe, who writhed with the head to seek for the pap, began again to cry afresh, whereby the poor man knew that it was a child, which by some sinister means was driven thither by distress of weather; marveling how such a silly infant, which by the mantle and the chain could not be but born of noble parentage, should be so hardly crossed with deadly mishap. The poor shepherd, perplexed thus with divers thoughts, took pity of the child, and determined with himself to carry it to the king, that there it might be brought up according to the worthiness of birth, for his ability could not afford to foster it, though his good mind was willing to further it. Taking therefore the child in his arms, as he folded the mantle together the better to defend it from cold there fell down at his foot a very fair and rich purse, wherein he found a great sum of gold; which sight so revived the shepherd's spirits, as he was greatly ravished with joy and daunted with fear; joyful to see such a sum in his power, and fearful, if it should be known, that it might breed his further danger. Necessity wished him at the least to retain the gold, though he would not keep the child: the simplicity of his conscience feared him from such deceitful bribery. Thus was the poor man perplexed with a doubtful dilemma until at last the covetousness of the coin overcame him; for what will not the greedy desire of gold cause a man to do? so that he was resolved in himself to foster the child, and with the sum to relieve his want. . . .

[He takes the child home, pacifies his suspicious wife, and swears her to secrecy. Later he buys the lease of a farm and stocks it with sheep, which Fawnia learns to tend.] . . . Fawnia thought Porrus had been her father and Mopsa her mother (for so was the shepherd and his wife called), honored and obeyed them with such reverence that all the neighbors praised the dutiful obedience of the child. Porrus grew in short time to be a man of some wealth and credit, for fortune so favored him in having no charge but Fawnia, that he began to purchase land, intending after his death to give it to his daughter, so that divers rich farmers' sons came as wooers to his house. For Fawnia was something cleanly attired, being of such singular beauty and excellent wit, that whoso saw her would have thought she had been some heavenly nymph and not a mortal creature, insomuch that, when she came to the age of sixteen years, she so increased with exquisite perfection both of body and mind, as her natural disposition did bewray that she was born of some high parentage; but the people thinking she was daughter to the shepherd Porrus rested only amazed at her beauty and wit; yea, she won such favor and commendations in every man's eye, as her beauty was not only praised in the country, but also spoken of in the court; yet such was her submiss modesty, that although her praise daily increased, her mind was no whit puffed up with pride, but humbled herself as became a country maid and the daughter of a poor shepherd. Every day she went forth with her sheep to the field, keeping them with such care and diligence

as all men thought she was very painful, defending her
face from the heat of the sun with no other veil but with
a garland made of boughs and flowers, which attire became
her so gallantly as she seemed to be the goddess Flora
herself for beauty. . . .

[Now we meet Dorastus (Florizel), who angers his
father by his unwillingness to marry.]

. . . It happened not long after this that there was a
meeting of all the farmers' daughters in Sicilia, whither
Fawnia was also bidden as the mistress of the feast, who,
having attired herself in her best garments, went among the
rest of her companions to the merry meeting, there spend-
ing the day in such homely pastimes as shepherds use. As
the evening grew on and their sports ceased, each taking
their leave at other, Fawnia, desiring one of her companions
to bear her company, went home by the flock to see if
they were well folded, and, as they returned, it fortuned
that Dorastus, who all that day had been hawking, and
killed store of game, encountered by the way these two
maids, and, casting his eye suddenly on Fawnia, he was
half afraid, fearing that with Actaeon he had seen Diana;
for he thought such exquisite perfection could not be
found in any mortal creature. As thus he stood in a maze,
one of his pages told him that the maid with the garland
on her head was Fawnia, the fair shepherd whose beauty
was so much talked of in the court. Dorastus, desirous to
see if nature had adorned her mind with any inward
qualities, as she had decked her body with outward shape,
began to question with her whose daughter she was, of
what age, and how she had been trained up? who answered
him with such modest reverence and sharpness of wit
that Dorastus thought her outward beauty was but a
counterfeit to darken her inward qualities, wondering
how so courtly behavior could be found in so simple a
cottage, and cursing fortune that had shadowed wit and
beauty with such hard fortune. As thus he held her a long
while with chat, beauty seeing him at discovert thought
not to lose the vantage, but struck him so deeply with an
envenomed shaft, as he wholly lost his liberty and became
a slave to love, which before contemned love, glad now

to gaze on a poor shepherd, who before refused the offer of a rich princess. . . .

[Dorastus laments his choice of a low-born girl; Fawnia knows he is above her station, but will not be his mistress. When he comes dressed as a shepherd and woos her honestly, she "yields up the fort."] . . . [Dorastus] embraced her in his arms, swearing that neither distance, time, nor adverse fortune should diminish his affection; but that, in despite of the destinies, he would remain loyal unto death. Having thus plighted their troth each to other, seeing they could not have the full fruition of their love in Sicilia, for that Egistus' consent would never be granted to so mean a match, Dorastus determined, as soon as time and opportunity would give them leave, to provide a great mass of money and many rich and costly jewels for the easier carriage, and then to transport themselves and their treasure into Italy, where they should lead a contented life, until such time as either he could be reconciled to his father, or else by succession come to the kingdom. . . .

[Fawnia approves the plan. The old shepherd (Porrus) gets wind of the affair and fears the king's anger. He discusses the problem with his wife.] . . . "If the king should know that Dorastus had begotten our daughter with child, as I fear it will fall out little better, the king's fury would be such as, no doubt, we should both lose our goods and lives. Necessity, therefore, hath no law, and I will prevent this mischief with a new device that is come in my head, which shall neither offend the king nor displease Dorastus. I mean to take the chain and the jewels that I found with Fawnia, and carry them to the king, letting him then to understand how she is none of my daughter, but that I found her beaten up with the water, alone in a little boat, wrapped in a rich mantle, wherein was enclosed this treasure. By this means, I hope the king will take Fawnia into his service, and we, whatsoever chanceth, shall be blameless." This device pleased the good wife very well, so that they determined, as soon as they might know the king at leisure, to make him privy to this case. . . .

[Capnio, Dorastus' old servant, completes preparations

for the lovers' flight, and gets them on board. The old shepherd sets out for the palace.] . . . He met by chance in his way Capnio, who, trudging as fast as he could with a little coffer under his arm to the ship, and spying Porrus, whom he knew to be Fawnia's father, going towards the palace, being a wily fellow, began to doubt the worst, and, therefore, crossed him by the way, and asked him whither he was going so early this morning? Porrus, who knew by his face that he was one of the court, meaning simply, told him that the king's son Dorastus dealt hardly with him, for he had but one daughter who was a little beautiful, and that the neighbors told him the young prince had allured her to folly: he went, therefore, now to complain to the king how greatly he was abused.

Capnio, who straightway smelt the whole matter, began to soothe him in his talk, and said that Dorastus dealt not like a prince to spoil any poor man's daughter in that sort: he, therefore, would do the best for him he could, because he knew he was an honest man. "But," quoth Capnio, "you lose your labor in going to the palace, for the king means this day to take the air of the sea, and to go aboard of a ship that lies in the haven. I am going before, you see, to provide all things in a readiness, and, if you will follow my counsel, turn back with me to the haven, where I will set you in such a fit place as you may speak to the king at your pleasure." Porrus, giving credit to Capnio's smooth tale, gave him a thousand thanks for his friendly advice and went with him to the haven, making all the way his complaints of Dorastus, yet concealing secretly the chain and the jewels. . . .

[Capnio forces the shepherd to board the lovers' ship. Dorastus is sought by his anxious father, who discovers the affair with Fawnia. Dorastus and Fawnia are driven by tempest to the Bohemian coast, and proceed to Pandosto's court.] . . . Pandosto, amazed at the singular perfection of Fawnia, stood half astonished, viewing her beauty, so that he had almost forgot himself what he had to do: at last, with stern countenance he demanded their names, and of what country they were, and what caused them to land in Bohemia. "Sir," quoth Dorastus, "know that my name Meleagrus is, a knight born and brought up in Trapolonia, and this gentlewoman, whom I mean to take to my wife, is an Italian, born in Padua, from whence I have now brought her. The cause I have so small a train with me is for that, her friends unwilling to consent, I intended secretly to convey her to Trapolonia; whither, as I was sailing by distress of weather I was driven into these coasts: thus have you heard my name, my country, and the cause of my voyage." Pandosto, starting from his seat as one in choler, made this rough reply:

"Meleagrus, I fear this smooth tale hath but small truth, and that thou coverest a foul skin with fair paintings. No doubt, this lady by her grace and beauty is of her degree more meet for a mighty prince than for a simple knight, and thou, like a perjured traitor, hath bereft her of her parents, to their present grief and her ensuing sorrow. Till, therefore, I hear more of her parentage and of thy calling I will stay you both here in Bohemia."

Dorastus, in whom rested nothing but kingly valor, was not able to suffer the reproaches of Pandosto, but that he made him this answer:

"It is not meet for a king, without due proof, to appeach any man of ill behavior, nor, upon suspicion, to infer belief: strangers ought to be entertained with courtesy, not to be entreated with cruelty, lest, being forced by want to put up injuries, the gods revenge their cause with rigor."

Pandosto, hearing Dorastus utter these words, commanded that he should straight be committed to prison, until such time as they heard further of his pleasure; but, as for Fawnia, he charged that she should be entertained in the court with such courtesy as belonged to a stranger and her calling. The rest of the shipmen he put into the dungeon.

Having, thus, hardly handled the supposed Trapolonians, Pandosto, contrary to his aged years, began to be somewhat tickled with the beauty of Fawnia. . . .

[Pandosto woos Fawnia, who resists him. Dorastus' father, hearing of the imprisonment of his son, sends an embassy to request his release and the execution of Fawnia

and the old shepherd. Pandosto consents, but the old
shepherd saves the situation by relating the discovery of
Fawnia.] . . . Pandosto would scarce suffer him to tell
out his tale but that he inquired the time of the year, the
manner of the boat, and other circumstances; which when
he found agreeing to his count, he suddenly leaped from
his seat and kissed Fawnia, wetting her tender cheeks
with his tears, and crying, "My daughter Fawnia! ah
sweet Fawnia! I am thy father, Fawnia." This sudden passion of the king drave them all into a maze, especially
Fawnia and Dorastus. But, when the king had breathed
himself a while in this new joy, he rehearsed before the
ambassadors the whole matter, how he had entreated his
wife Bellaria for jealousy, and that this was the child, whom
he had sent to float in the seas. . . .

[Great rejoicing follows. Then . . .] Pandosto, willing
to recompense old Porrus, of a shepherd made him a
knight; which done, providing a sufficient navy to receive
him and his retinue, accompanied with Dorastus, Fawnia,
and the Sicilian ambassadors, he sailed towards Sicilia,
where he was most princely entertained by Egistus; who,
hearing this most comical event, rejoiced greatly at his
son's good hap, and without delay (to the perpetual joy
of the two young lovers) celebrated the marriage: which
was no sooner ended, but Pandosto, calling to mind how
first he betrayed his friend Egistus, how his jealousy was
the cause of Bellaria's death, that contrary to the law of
nature he had lusted after his own daughter, moved with
these desperate thoughts, he fell into a melancholy fit, and,
to close up the comedy with a tragical stratagem, he slew
himself. . . .

Commentaries

Simon Forman

The Winter's Tale at the Globe, 1611, the 15 of May

Observe there how Leontes, the King of Sicilia, was overcome with jealousy of his wife with the King of Bohemia his friend, that came to see him; and how he contrived his death and would have had his cupbearer to have poisoned, who gave the King of Bohemia warning thereof and fled with him to Bohemia.

Remember also how he sent to the Oracle of Apollo, and the answer of Apollo, that she was guiltless and that the King was jealous, etc., and how except the child was found again that was lost, the King should die without issue; for the child was carried into Bohemia and there laid in a forest and brought up by a shepherd. And the King of Bohemia his son married that wench, and how they fled into Sicilia to Leontes, and the shepherd having showed the letter of the nobleman by whom Leontes sent away that

From Forman's *Booke of Plaies*.

child and the jewels found about her, she was known to be Leontes' daughter, and was then sixteen years old.

Remember also the Rogue that came in all tattered like coll pixci,[1] and how he feigned him sick and to have been robbed of all that he had, and how he cozened the poor man of all his money, and after came to the sheep-shear with a peddler's pack, and there cozened them again of all their money. And how he changed apparel with the King of Bohemia his son, and then how he turned courtier, etc. Beware of trusting feigned beggars or fawning fellows.

[1] A doubtful reading, of doubtful significance.

Samuel Taylor Coleridge

[Comments on *The Winter's Tale*]

At the commencement of the fourth lecture last evening,
Mr. Coleridge combated the opinion held by some critics,
that the writings of Shakespeare were like a wilderness,
in which were desolate places, most beautiful flowers, and
weeds; he argued that even the titles of his plays were
appropriate and showed judgment, presenting as it were
a bill of fare before the feast. This was peculiarly so in
The Winter's Tale—a wild story, calculated to interest
a circle round a fireside. He maintained that Shakespeare
ought not to be judged of in detail, but on the whole. A
pedant differed from a master in cramping himself with
certain established rules, whereas the master regarded
rules as always controllable by and subservient to the end.
The passion to be delineated in *The Winter's Tale* was
jealousy. Shakespeare's description of this, however, was
perfectly philosophical: the mind, in its first harboring of

In 1813–14 Coleridge delivered a series of lectures at Bristol. They
do not survive, but the reports of them in the *Bristol Gazette* provide
an idea of their gist. The first passage contains all that was reported of
the lecture on *The Winter's Tale*. The scrappier material printed beneath
this report is from Coleridge's marginalia. All of this Coleridge material
is drawn from 2nd ed., ed. Thomas Middleton Raysor. New York: E. P.
Dutton & Company, Inc., 1960; London: J. M. Dent & Sons, Ltd., 1961.
2 vols.

it, became mean and despicable, and the first sensation
was perfect shame, arising from the consideration of having
possessed an object unworthily, of degrading a person to
a thing. The mind that once indulges this passion has a
predisposition, a vicious weakness, by which it kindles a
fire from every spark, and from circumstances the most
innocent and indifferent finds fuel to feed the flame. This
he exemplified in an able manner from the conduct and
opinion of Leontes, who seized upon occurrences of which
he himself was the cause, and when speaking of Hermione,
combined his anger with images of the lowest sensuality,
and pursued the object with the utmost cruelty. This
character Mr. Coleridge contrasted with that of Othello,
whom Shakespeare had portrayed the very opposite to a
jealous man: he was noble, generous, open-hearted; un-
suspicious and unsuspecting.

*   *   *

Although on the whole exquisitely respondent to its title,
and even in the fault I am about to mention, still a winter's
tale, yet it seems a mere indolence of the great bard not
to have in the oracle provided some ground for Hermione's
seeming death and fifteen years concealment, voluntary
concealment. This might have been easily affected by some
obscure sentence of the oracle, as, *ex. gr.,* "Nor shall he
ever recover an heir if he have a wife before that recovery."

[IV.iv.445–54]

Perdita.   Even here undone!
  I was not much afeard; for once or twice
  I was about to speak and tell him plainly,
  The selfsame sun that shines upon his court
  Hides not his visage from our cottage, but
  Looks on alike. [*To Florizel*] Will 't please you, sir,
    be gone?
  I told you what would come of this. Beseech you,
  Of your own state take care: this dream of mine
  Being now awake, I'll queen it no inch farther,
  But milk my ewes, and weep.]

O how more than exquisite is this whole speech,—and that profound nature of noble pride and grief venting themselves in a momentary peevishness of resentment toward Florizel—

> Will 't please you, sir, be gone?

Difference of style in the first scene between two chitchatters [Camillo and Archidamus], and the rise of diction on the introduction of the kings and Hermione [in the second scene].

Admirable preparation in Polixenes' obstinate refusal to Leontes—

> There is no tongue that moves, none, none i' th' world

and yet his after-yielding to Hermione, which is at once perfectly natural from mere courtesy of sex and the exhaustion of the will by the former effort, and yet so well calculated to set in nascent action the jealousy of Leontes. And this, once excited, [is] increased by Hermione—

> yet, good deed, Leontes,
> [I love thee not a jar o' th' clock behind
> What lady she her lord]

accompanied (as a good actress ought to represent it) by an expression and recoil of apprehension that she had gone too far. The first working of this—

> At my request he would not.

This [should be] judiciously introduced accompanied by a definition of *jealousy,* not of all so-called by persons imperfectly acquainted with the circumstances, but of what really is so; i.e., [jealousy] as a *vice* of the mind, a culpable despicable tendency.

The natural effects and concomitants of this passion.

1. Excitability by the most inadequate causes [as in Leontes' aside], "Too hot, too hot." Eagerness to snatch at proofs. . . .

2. Grossness of conception, and a disposition to degrade the object of it. Sensual fancies and images. . . .

3. Shame of his own feelings exhibited in moodiness and soliloquy.

4. And yet from the violence of the passion forced to *utter* itself, and, therefore, catching occasion to ease the mind by ambiguities, equivoques, talking to those who cannot and who are known not to be able to understand what is said—a soliloquy in the mask of dialogue. [I.ii.120–27]. Hence confused, broken manner, fragmentary, in the dialogue with the little boy.

5. The dread of vulgar ridicule, as distinct from the high sense of honor—

> They're here with me already: whispering, rounding [I.ii.217].

and out of this, selfish vindictiveness. How distinguished from the feeling of high honor (as in Othello), a mistaken sense of duty.

E. M. W. Tillyard

From *Shakespeare's Last Plays*

In *The Winter's Tale* Shakespeare omitted all the irrelevancies that had clotted *Cymbeline* and presented the whole tragic pattern, from prosperity to destruction, regeneration, and still fairer prosperity, in full view of the audience. This is a bold, frontal attack on the problem, necessitating the complete disregard of the unity of time; but it succeeded, as far as success was possible within the bounds of a single play. One difference in plot from *Cymbeline* is that there is little overlap between the old and the new life. In Guiderius and Arviragus the new life had been incubating for years while the old life held sway in Cymbeline and his court. But Perdita, chief symbol of the new life, has not lived many hours before Leontes begins his own conversion.

Unlike *Cymbeline,* the first half of the play is seriously tragic and could have included Hermione's death, like Greene's *Pandosto.* Leontes's obsession of jealousy is terrifying in its intensity. It reminds us not of other Shakespearian tragic errors, but rather of the god-sent lunacies

From *Shakespeare's Last Plays* by E. M. W. Tillyard. London: Chatto & Windus, Ltd., 1938; New York: Hillary House Publishers, Ltd. Reprinted by permission of Chatto & Windus, Ltd.

of Greek drama, the lunacies of Ajax and Heracles. It is as scantily motivated as these, and we should refrain from demanding any motive. Indeed, it is as much a surprise to the characters in the play as it is to the reader, and its nature is that of an earthquake or the loss of the *Titanic* rather than of rational human psychology. And equally terrifying is Leontes's cry, when, after defying the oracle, he hears of his son's death:

> Apollo's angry; and the heavens themselves
> Do strike at my injustice.

Hermione's character is far more firmly based on probability than Imogen's. There is nothing strained or hectic about her love for her husband: it is rooted in habit. And when at her trial, addressing Leontes, she says:

> To me can life be no commodity;
> The crown and comfort of my life, your favor,
> I do give lost; for I do feel it gone,
> But know not how it went,

we accept the statement as sober truth. While for distilled pathos no poet, not even Euripides, has excelled her final soliloquy, when she realizes Leontes's fixed hostility:

> The Emperor of Russia was my father:
> O that he were alive, and here beholding
> His daughter's trial! that he did but see
> The flatness of my misery, yet with eyes
> Of pity, not revenge!

In sum, the first half of the play renders worthily, in the main through a realistic method, the destructive portion of the tragic pattern.

Now, although Leontes and Hermione live on to give continuity to the play and although the main tragic pattern is worked out nominally in Leontes, the royal person, it is not they in their reconciliation who most create the feeling of rebirth. At the best they mend the broken vessel of their fortunes with glue or seccotine; and our imaginations are not in the least stirred by any future life that we can conceive the pair enjoying together. Were the pattern of destruction and regeneration the sole motive of the play, the statue scene would have little point and be, as Middleton Murry calls it, a theatrical trick. But the continued existence of Leontes and Hermione is a matter of subordinate expediency; and it is Florizel and Perdita and the countryside where they meet which make the new life.

And here I must plead as earnestly as I can for allowing more than the usual virtue and weight to the fourth act of *The Winter's Tale*. There are several reasons why it has been taken too lightly. It has been far too much the property of vague young women doing eurythmics at Speech Days or on vicarage lawns; and, when it is acted professionally, the part of Perdita is usually taken by some pretty little fool or pert suburban charmer. Also, it is usually thought that joy and virtue are inferior as poetic themes to suffering and vice; or that the earthly paradise taxed the resources of Dante less than Ugolino's tower. It would seem that the truth is the other way round, because convincing pictures of joy and virtue are extremely rare, while those of suffering and vice are comparatively common. Shelley succeeds in describing the sufferings of Prometheus; the earthly bliss brought on by them is, except in patches, a shoddy affair in comparison. Shakespeare never did anything finer, more serious, more evocative of his full powers, than his picture of an earthly paradise painted in the form of the English countryside. The old problem of adjusting realism and symbol is so well solved that we are quite unconscious of it. The country life is given the fullest force of actuality, as when the old shepherd describes his wife's hospitality at the shearing feast:

Fie, daughter! when my old wife lived, upon
This day she was both pantler, butler, cook,
Both dame and servant; welcomed all, served all:
Would sing her song and dance her turn; now here,

At upper end o' the table, now i' the middle;
On his shoulder, and his; her face o' fire
With labor and the thing she took to quench it,
She would to each one sip.

Yet the whole country setting stands out as the cleanest and most elegant symbol of the new life into which the old horrors are to be transmuted.

It is the same with the characters. Shakespeare blends the realistic and the symbolic with the surest touch. Florizel, who is kept a rather flat character the more to show up Perdita, one would call a type rather than a symbol; but for the play's purposes he is an efficient type of chivalry and generosity. He will not let down Perdita, but defies his father at the risk of losing a kingdom:

I am not sorry, not afeard; delay'd
But nothing altered: what I was, I am;
More straining on for plucking back, not following
My leash unwillingly.

Perdita, on the other hand, is one of Shakespeare's richest characters; at once a symbol and a human being. She is the play's main symbol of the powers of creation. And rightly, because, as Leontes was the sole agent of destruction, so it is fitting, ironically fitting, that the one of his kin whom he had thrown out as bastard should embody the contrary process. Not that Leontes, as a character, is the contrary to Perdita. His obsession is not a part of his character but an accretion. Her true contrary is Iago. It is curious that Iago should ever have been thought motiveless. The desire to destroy is a very simple derivative from the power instinct, the instinct which in its evil form goes by the name of the first of the deadly sins, Pride. It was by that sin that the angels fell, and at the end of *Othello* Iago is explicitly equated with the Devil. Shakespeare embodied all his horror of this type of original sin in Iago. He was equally aware of original virtue, and he pictured it, in Perdita, blossoming spontaneously in the

simplest of country settings. There is little direct reference
to her instincts to create; but they are implied by her
sympathy with nature's lavishness in producing flowers,
followed by her own simple and unashamed confession
of wholesome sensuality. The whole passage, so often
confined to mere idyllic description, must be quoted in
hopes that the reader will allow the profounder significance
I claim for it. Perdita is talking to her guests, to Polixenes,
Camillo, and Florizel in particular:

> *Perdita.* Here's flowers for you;
>   Hot lavender, mints, savory, marjoram;
>   The Marigold, that goes to bed wi' the sun
>   And with him rises weeping: these are flowers
>   Of middle summer, and I think they are given
>   To men of middle age. You're very welcome.
>
> *Camillo.* I should leave grazing, were I of your flock,
>   And only live by gazing.
>
> *Perdita.*   Out, alas!
>   You'd be so lean, that blasts of January
>   Would blow you through and through. Now, my
>   fair'st friend,
>   I would I had some flowers o' the spring that might
>   Become your time of day; and yours, and yours,
>   That wear upon your virgin branches yet
>   Your maidenheads growing: O Proserpina,
>   For the flowers now, that frighted thou let'st fall
>   From Dis's wagon! daffodils,
>   That come before the swallow dares, and take
>   The winds of March with beauty; violets dim,
>   But sweeter than the lids of Juno's eyes
>   Or Cytherea's breath; pale primroses,
>   That die unmarried, ere they can behold
>   Bright Phoebus in his strength—a malady
>   Most incident to maids; bold oxlips and
>   The crown imperial; lilies of all kinds,
>   The flower-de-luce being one! O, these I lack,
>   To make you garlands of, and my sweet friend,
>   To strew him o'er and o'er.

Florizel.   What, like a corse?

Perdita. No, like a bank for love to lie and play on;
   Not like a corse; or if, not to be buried,
   But quick and in mine arms.

The great significance of Perdita's lines lies partly in the
verse, which (especially at the close) is leisurely, full,
assured, matured, suggestive of fruition, and acutely contrasted to the tortured, arid, and barren ravings of Leontes,
and which reinforces that kinship with nature and healthy
sensuality mentioned above. But it lies also in the references to the classical Pantheon. The gods of Greece and
Rome occur very frequently in the last plays of Shakespeare and are certainly more than mere embroidery.
Apollo is the dominant god in *The Winter's Tale,* and his
appearance in Perdita's speech is meant to quicken the
reader to apprehend some unusual significance. He appears as the bridegroom, whom the pale primroses never
know, but who visits the other flowers. Not to take the
fertility symbolism as intended would be a perverse act
of caution. Perdita should be associated with them, as
symbol both of the creative powers of nature, physical
fertility, and of healing and re-creation of the mind. She
is like Milton's youthful Ceres,

          Yet virgin of Proserpina from Jove,

or his Eve, mistress of the flowers of Paradise.

   The health of Perdita's natural instincts not only helps
her symbolic force; it helps to make her a realistic
character. Other parts of her character are a deep-seated
strength and ruthless common sense. She argues coolly
with Polixenes about art and nature, and is not frightened
by his later fulminations, saying when he has gone:

      I was not much afeard; for once or twice
      I was about to speak and tell him plainly,
      The selfsame sun that shines upon his court
      Hides not his visage from our cottage but
      Looks on alike.

At the same time she shows that she has been all the time quite without illusions about the danger she runs in loving Florizel, the Prince, and when the shock comes with the discovery of their plighted love she is prepared without fuss to accept her fate. Turning to Florizel, she goes on:

> Will't please you, sir, be gone?
> I told you what would come of this: beseech you,
> Of your own state take care: this dream of mine—
> Being now awake, I'll queen it no inch farther,
> But milk my ewes and weep.

It is through Perdita's magnificence that we accept as valuable the new life into which the play is made to issue. The disadvantage of centering the creative processes in her and Florizel is structural. There is a break in continuity; for though Perdita is born in the first half of the play, as characters the pair are new to the last half. And we have juxtaposition, not organic growth. There is no Orestes to lead from the *Choephoroe* to the *Eumenides*. On the other hand, I find this juxtaposition easy enough to accept; and it is mitigated by Perdita's parentage. She is Hermione's true daughter and prolongs in herself those regenerative processes which in her mother have suffered a temporary eclipse.

The common praise of Autolycus as a character is well justified. It is likely that he is organic to the whole country scene, and that it would collapse into an oversweetness of sentiment without him. Though he comes and goes with the aloofness of an elf among humans, he is united with the other characters in his admirable adjustment to the country life. His delinquencies, like the pastoral realism, keep the earthly paradise sufficiently earthly without disturbing the paradisiac state; for they are antitoxic, harmless to vigorous health, and an efficient prophylactic against the lotus fruit which, as a drug, has so greatly impaired the health of most earthly paradises.

* * * * * *

If *The Winter's Tale* succeeded better than *Cymbeline*

with the tragic pattern, so did it with the planes of reality
also. No blurring, but clean contrast. The paranoiac world
of Leontes is set against the everyday world of the courtiers
and the world, still of everyday but intensified, of Hermione. Leontes's world is marvelously expressed by the
hot and twisted language he uses. Another world is introduced at the beginning of the third act by the short
scene where Cleomenes and Dion speak of their visit to
the Oracle. Here the words are cool and pellucid: we are
in the realm of contemplation.

> *Cleomenes.* The climate's delicate, the air most sweet,
>   Fertile the isle, the temple much surpassing
>   The common praise it bears.
>
> *Dion.*   I shall report,
>   For most it caught me, the celestial habits,
>   Methinks I so should term them, and the reverence
>   Of the grave wearers. O, the sacrifice!
>   How ceremonious, solemn, and unearthly
>   It was i' the offering.

And this "ceremonious, solemn, and unearthly" note is
repeated in the great scene, in itself fantastically unreal,
where Leontes kisses Hermione's statue and it comes to life.
It would be tedious to speak of every transition in this play
from one world to another. I will confine myself to noting
the most violent of all, and one which the greatest skeptic
of my argument would hardly consider accidental. Antigonus, on the coast of Bohemia, carrying the infant Perdita,
sends the mariner back to his ship and proceeds to describe
in a soliloquy how Hermione appeared to him in a dream.
There is nothing in the play so melodramatic, so remote
from ordinary life as this speech:

>   She did approach
>   My cabin where I lay; thrice bow'd before me,
>   And gasping to begin some speech, her eyes
>   Became two spouts: the fury spent, anon
>   Did this break from her—

and when she had done speaking, "with shrieks she melted
into air." From this strained, impossible world we are
abruptly recalled by the stage direction *exit, pursued by a
bear*, and the entry of the old shepherd, whose first words
put us at the very center of common humanity:

> I would there were no age between ten-and-three-
> and-twenty, or that youth would sleep out the rest; for
> there is nothing in the between but getting wenches with
> child, wronging the ancientry, stealing, fighting.

It is worth noting, in parenthesis, that the above abrupt
transition not only expresses the sense of different worlds
but has an important technical work to do, that of throwing
a bridge across the two halves of the play. Shakespeare
has to present us in the country scenes with a new kind of
serious writing, with re-creation after destruction. Now it
is easy enough to set the farcical or the grotesque against
tragedy without fear of misunderstanding. But to set the
serious world of Perdita abruptly against the other serious
world of Leontes and Hermione might make trouble. Perdita might appear too slight, set against the earlier violence.
Shakespeare's solution is to drive the tortured world of
Leontes and Hermione to a ridiculous extreme in Antigonus' vision. In so doing he really puts an end to it. Any
return to it would court ridicule. But the ridiculousness of
Antigonus' vision prepares us for any kind of the ridiculous; and Shakespeare proceeds to give us good earthy
comedy, and we take it. Out of this comedy grows the
serious, sane, and transfigured earthiness of the Perdita
scenes, which we now never dream of confusing with the
world of Leontes and Hermione. This transition has obvious analogies with music.

G. Wilson Knight

From *The Crown of Life*

[Mr. Knight uses as his text IV.iv. 79–112.] Of this one could say much. Notice first, the continued emphasis on seasons at the opening and concluding lines of my quotation; the strong physical realism (recalling Hermione's defense) in Perdita's use of "breed"; and the phrase "great creating nature" (to be compared with "great nature" earlier, at II.ii.59).

The speakers are at cross purposes, since one is referring to art, the other to artificiality, itself a difficult enough distinction. The whole question of the naturalist and transcendental antinomy is accordingly raised. The art concerned is called natural by Polixenes in that either (i) human invention can never do more than direct natural energy, or (ii) the human mind and therefore its inventions are nature-born: both meanings are probably contained. Human civilization, art and religion are clearly in one sense part of "great creating nature," and so is everything else. But Perdita takes her stand on natural simplicity, growing from the unforced integrity of her own country upbringing, in opposition to the artificialities of, we may

From *The Crown of Life* by G. Wilson Knight, 2nd. ed. London: Methuen & Co., Ltd., 1948; New York: British Book Centre, 1952. Reprinted by permission of Methuen & Co., Ltd.

suggest, the court: she is horrified at dishonoring nature by
human trickery. Observe that both alike reverence "great
creating nature," though differing in their conclusions. No
logical deduction is to be drawn; or rather, the logic is
dramatic, made of opposing statements, which serve to
conjure up an awareness of nature as an all-powerful
presence, at once controller and exemplar. The dialogue
forms accordingly a microcosm of our whole drama.

There is a certain irony, too, in Polixenes' defense of
exactly the type of love-mating which Florizel and Perdita are planning for themselves. Polixenes is, perhaps,
setting a trap; or may be quite unconsciously arguing
against his own later behavior. Probably the latter.

Perdita next turns to Florizel:

> *Perdita.*   Now, my fair'st friend,
> I would I had some flowers o' the spring that might
> Become your time of day; and yours, and yours,
> That wear upon your virgin branches yet
> Your maidenheads growing: O Proserpina!
> For the flowers now that frighted thou let'st fall
> From Dis's wagon! daffodils
> That come before the swallow dares, and take
> The winds of March with beauty; violets dim,
> But sweeter than the lids of Juno's eyes
> Or Cytherea's breath; pale primroses
> That die unmarried ere they can behold
> Bright Phoebus in his strength, a malady
> Most incident to maids; bold oxlips and
> The crown imperial; lilies of all kinds,
> The flower-de-luce being one. O! these I lack
> To make you garlands of, and my sweet friend,
> To strew him o'er and o'er!
>
> *Florizel.*   What! like a corse?
>
> *Perdita.* No, like a bank for love to lie and play on;
> Not like a corse; or if—not to be buried,
> But quick and in mine arms. Come, take your
>   flowers:
> Methinks I play as I have seen them do

> In Whitsun pastorals: sure this robe of mine
> Does change my disposition.
>
> (IV.iv.112)

Reference to the season-myth of Proserpine is natural
enough; indeed, almost an essential. You might call Perdita herself a seed sowed in winter and flowering in
summer. "Take" = "charm," or "enrapture." Though
Autolycus' first entry suggested spring, we are already, as
the nature of our festival and these lines declare, in summer. Note the fine union, indeed identity, of myth and
contemporary experience, finer than in earlier Shakespearian pastorals: Dis may be classical, but his "wagon"
is as real as a wagon in Hardy. See, too, how classical
legend and folklore coalesce in the primroses and "bright
Phoebus in his strength," a phrase pointing the natural
poetic association of sun fire and mature love (as in
Antony and Cleopatra): the sun corresponding, as it
were, to physical fruition (as the moon to the more operatic
business of wooing) and accordingly raising in Perdita,
whose poetry is strongly impregnated with fertility suggestion (the magic here is throughout an earth magic, a sun
magic), a wistful aside, meant presumably for herself.
Perdita's flower poetry reaches a royal impressionism in
"crown imperial" and "garland" suiting the speaker's
innate, and indeed actual, royalty. The contrasting suggestion of "corse" quickly merging into a love embrace
(reminiscent of the love and death associations in *Antony
and Cleopatra* and Keats) finally serves to heighten the
pressure of exuberant, buoyant, life. The "Whitsun pastorals," like our earlier puritans, though perhaps histori-
cally extraneous, may be forgiven for their lively impact,
serving to render the speech vivid with the poet's, and
hence, somehow, our own, personal experience.

Perdita's royalty is subtly presented: her robes as mistress of the feast have, as she said, made her act and
speak strangely. Florizel details each of her graces (IV.
iv.135–43), wishing her in turn to speak, to sing, to
dance—as "a wave o' the sea"—forever. He would have

her every action perpetuated, the thought recalling Polixenes' recollections of himself and Leontes as "boy eternal" (I.ii.65). Florizel has expressed a delight in the given instant of youthful grace so sacred that it somehow deserves eternal status; when she moves he would have her, in a phrase itself patterning the blend of motion and stillness it describes, "move still, still so." Watching her, he sees the universe completed, crowned, at each moment of her existence:

> Each your doing,
> So singular in each particular,
> Crowns what you are doing in the present deeds
> That all your acts are queens.
>
> (IV.iv.143)

As once before, we are reminded, this time more sharply, of Blake's "minute particulars." The royalistic tonings here and in the "crown imperial" of her own speech (IV.iv.126) not merely hint Perdita's royal blood, but also serve to stamp her actions with eternal validity; for the crown is always to be understood as a symbol piercing the eternity dimension. We are, it is true, being forced into distinctions that Shakespeare, writing from a royalistic age, need not actually have surveyed; but Florizel's lines certainly correspond closely to those in *Pericles* imaging Marina as a palace "for the crown'd Truth to dwell in" and again as monumental Patience sitting "above kings' graves" and "smiling extremity out of act" (*Pericles,* V.i. 123, 140). Perdita is more lively; time, creation, nature, earth, all have more rights here than in *Pericles*; but the correspondence remains close.

Perdita's acts are royal both in their own right and also because she is, in truth, of royal birth:

> This is the prettiest low-born lass that ever
> Ran on the greensward. Nothing she does or seems
> But smacks of something greater than herself,
> Too noble for this place.
>
> (IV.iv.156)

But this is not the whole truth. Later, after Polixenes'
outburst, she herself makes a comment more easily appre-
ciated in our age than in Shakespeare's:

> I was not much afeard; for once or twice
> I was about to speak and tell him plainly,
> The selfsame sun that shines upon his court
> Hides not his visage from our cottage, but
> Looks on alike.

(IV.iv.446)

The lovely New Testament transposition (with "sun" for
"rain") serves to underline the natural excellence and
innate worth of this simple rustic community; and only
from some such recognition can we make full sense of the
phrase "queen of curds and cream" (IV.iv.161). We may
accordingly regroup our three royalties in terms of (i)
Perdita's actual descent, (ii) her natural excellence and
(iii) that more inclusive category from which both descend,
or to which both aspire, in the eternity-dimension. A final
conclusion would reach some concept of spiritual royalty
corresponding to Wordsworth's (in his *Immortality Ode*);
with further political implications concerning the expansion of sovereignty among a people.

The lovers are, very clearly, felt as creatures of "rare"
—the expected word recurs (IV.iv.32)—excellence, and
their love, despite its strong fertility contacts, is corres-
pondingly pure. Perdita, hearing Florizel's praises, fears
he woos her "the false way" (IV.iv.151); while Florizel is
equally insistent that his "desires run not before his
honor," nor his "lusts burn hotter" than his "faith" (IV.
iv.33). The statement, which appears, as in *The Tempest*
later, a trifle labored, is clearly central: Perdita, as mistress of the feast, insists that Autolycus "use no scurrilous
words in's tunes" (IV.iv.215). Our first tragedy was pre-
cipitated by suspicion of marital infidelity; and our young
lovers express a corresponding purity. . . .

. . . Now, as the resurrection draws near, we are prepared for it by Perdita's restoration. St. Paul once seems,
perhaps justly, to consider resurrection as no more remarkable than birth (see Romans 4:17 in Dr. Moffatt's trans-

lation).[1] Certainly here the safeguarding of Perdita is considered scarcely less wonderful than the resurrection of the dead. That the child should be found, says Paulina,

> Is all as monstrous to our *human reason*
> As my Antigonus to break his grave
> And come again to me.
>
>   (V.i.41)

Yet she is restored, as the Gentlemen recount, and human reason accordingly negated. Scattered throughout are dim foreshadowings of the miraculous. Nevertheless, death looms large enough still, in poetry's despite: Paulina sees to that. When a gentleman praises Perdita she remarks:

> O Hermione!
> As every present time doth boast itself
> Above a better gone, so must thy grave
> Give way to what's seen now.
>
>   (V.i.95)

The temporal order demands that the past slip away, that it lose reality; the more visible present always seems *superior*. Paulina resents this; and her remark may be aligned with both our early lines on boyhood never dreaming of any future other than to be "boy eternal" (I.ii.65) and Florizel's desire to have Perdita's every act in turn—speaking, dancing, etc.—perpetuated. All these are strivings after eternity. Paulina, moreover, here suggests that the gentleman concerned, who seems to be a poet, is himself at fault: his verse, which "flow'd with her [i.e., Hermione's] beauty once," is now "shrewdly ebb'd" (V.i. 102). The complaint is, not that Hermione has gone, but that the gentleman has failed in some sense to keep level. Death is accordingly less an objective reality than a failure of the subject to keep abreast of life. This may seem to turn an obvious thought into meaningless metaphysics, but the lines, in their context, can scarcely be ignored. Throughout *Troilus and Cressida* (especially at III.iii.145–84, an

---

[1] It must, however, be noted that the birth here concerned seems to be one of an abnormal, semimiraculous, sort; but the Pauline doctrine of resurrection holds strong fertility suggestion elsewhere, as in the great passage on immortality at 1 Corinthians, XV, where the dead body is compared to a grain of wheat buried in earth.

expansion of Paulina's comment) Shakespeare's thoughts
on time are highly abstruse (see my essay in *The Wheel of
Fire*); so are they in the Sonnets. Wrongly used time is as
intrinsic to the structure of *Macbeth* as is "eternity" to
that of *Antony and Cleopatra* (see my essays on both plays
in *The Imperial Theme*). As so often in great poetry, the
philosophical subtlety exists within or behind a speech,
or plot, of surface realism and simplicity. Now *The Winter's Tale* is hammering on the threshold of some extraordinary truth related to both "nature" and "eternity."
Hence its emphasis on the seasons, birth and childhood,
the continual molding of new miracles on the pattern of
the old; hence, too, the desire expressed for youthful
excellence perpetuated and eternal; the thought of Perdita's every action as a "crowned" thing, a "queen," in its
own eternal right (IV.iv.145–6); and also of art as improving or distorting nature, in the flower-dialogue, in
Julio Romano's uncanny, eternity-imitating, skill. And yet
no metaphysics, no natural philosophy or art, satisfy the
demand that the lost thing, in all its nature-born warmth,
be preserved; that it, not only its descendant, shall live;
that death be revealed as a sin-born illusion; that eternity
be flesh and blood.

The action moves to the house of the "grave and good
Paulina" (V.iii.1). The scene is her "chapel," recalling the
chapel of death at III.ii.237, where Leontes last saw
Hermione's dead body. Paulina shows them the statue,
which excels anything "the hand of man hath done" (V.
iii.17); and they are quickly struck with—again the word
—"wonder" (V.iii.22). Leontes gazes; recognizes Hermione's "natural posture" (V.iii.23); asks her to chide him,
yet remembers how she was tender "as infancy and grace"
(V.iii.27):

>   O! thus she stood,
> Even with such life of majesty—warm life
> As now it coldly stands—when first I woo'd her.
> I am asham'd: does not the stone rebuke me
> For being more stone than it? O, royal piece!
>   (V.iii.34)

Sweet though it be, it remains cold and withdrawn, like
Keats' Grecian Urn. Yet its "majesty" exerts a strangely
potent "magic" (V.iii.39) before which Perdita kneels
almost in "superstition" (V.iii.43). Leontes' grief is so
great that Camillo reminds him how "sixteen winters"
and "so many summers" should by now alternately have
blown and dried his soul clean of "sorrow"; why should that
prove more persistent than short-lived "joy"? (V.iii.49–53).
Leontes remains still, his soul pierced (V.iii.34)
by remembrance. Paulina, however, speaks realistically of
the statue as art, saying how its color is not dry yet (V.
iii.47); half apologizing for the way it moves him, her
phrase "for the stone is mine" (V.iii.58) re-emphasizing
her peculiar office. She offers to draw the curtain, fearing
lest Leontes' "fancy may think anon it moves" (V.iii.60–
61). The excitement generated, already intense, reaches
new impact and definition in Paulina's sharp ringing utterance on "moves."

But Leontes remains quiet, fixed, in an otherworldly
consciousness, a living death not to be disturbed, yet
trembling with expectance:

> Let be, let be!
> Would I were dead, but that, methinks, already—
> What was he that did make it?
>
> (V.iii.61)

A universe of meaning is hinted by that one word "already"
and the subsequent, tantalizing, break. Now the statue
seems no longer cold:

> See, my lord,
> Would you not deem it breath'd, and that those veins
> Did verily bear blood?
>
> (V.iii.63)

As the revelation slowly matures, it is as though Leontes'
own grief and love were gradually infusing the thing before him with life. He, under Paulina, is laboring, even
now, that it may live. The more visionary, paradisal, personal wonder of Pericles (who alone hears the spheral
music) becomes here a crucial conflict, an *agon,* in which
many persons share; dream is being forced into actuality.

"Masterly done," answers Polixenes, taking us back to common sense, and yet again noting that "the very life seems warm upon her lip" (V.iii.65). We are poised between motion and stillness, life and art:

> The fixture of her eye has motion in't
> As we are mock'd with art.
>
> (V.iii.67)

The contrast drives deep, recalling the balancing of art and nature in Perdita's dialogue with Polixenes; and, too, the imaging of the living Marina as "crown'd Truth" or monumental Patience (*Pericles*, V.i.124,140). Paulina reiterates her offer to draw the curtain lest Leontes be so far "transported" (cf. III.ii.155; a word strongly toned in Shakespeare with magical suggestion) that he actually think it "lives"—thus recharging the scene with an impossible expectation. To which Leontes replies:

> No settled senses of the world can match
> The pleasure of that madness. Let't alone.
>
> (V.iii.72)

He would stand here, spellbound, forever; forever gazing on this sphinxlike boundary between art and life.

Paulina, having functioned throughout as the Oracle's implement, becomes now its priestess. Her swift changes key the scene to an extraordinary pitch, as she hints at new marvels:

> I am sorry, sir, I have thus far stirr'd you: but
> I could afflict you further.   (V.iii.74)

She has long caused, and still causes, Leontes to suffer poignantly; and yet his suffering has undergone a subtle change, for now this very "affliction has a taste as sweet as any cordial comfort" (V.iii.76). Already (at V.ii.20 and 78, and V.iii.51–3) we have found joy and sorrow in partnership, as, too, in the description of Cordelia's grief (*King Lear*, IV.iii.17–26). So Leontes endures a pain of ineffable sweetness as the mystery unfolds:

> Still, methinks,
> There is an air comes from her: what fine chisel
> Could ever yet cut breath?   (V.iii.77)

However highly we value the eternity phrased by art (as in Yeats' "monuments of unaging intellect" in "Sailing to Byzantium" [2] and Keats' "Grecian Urn"), yet there is a frontier beyond which it and all corresponding philosophies fail: they lack one thing, breath. With a fine pungency of phrase, more humanly relevant that Othello's "I know not where is that Promethean heat. . . ." (*Othello*, V.ii. 12), a whole world of human idealism is dismissed. The supreme moments of earlier tragedy—Othello before the "monumental alabaster" (V.ii.5) of the sleeping Desdemona, Romeo in Capulet's monument, Juliet and Cleopatra blending sleep and death—are implicit in Leontes' experience; more, their validity is at stake, as he murmurs, "Let no man mock me" (V.iii.79), stepping forward for an embrace; as old Lear, reunited with Cordelia, "a spirit in bliss," says "Do not laugh at me" (*King Lear*, IV.vii. 68); as Pericles fears lest his reunion with Marina be merely such a dream as "mocks" man's grief (*Pericles*, V.i.144,164). Those, and other, supreme moments of pathos are here re-enacted to a stronger purpose. Leontes strides forward; is prevented by Paulina; we are brought up against a cul-de-sac. But Paulina herself immediately releases new impetus as she cries, her voice quivering with the Sibylline power she wields:

> Either forbear,
> Quit presently the chapel, or resolve you
> For more amazement. If you can behold it,
> I'll make the statue move indeed, descend,
> And take you by the hand; but then you'll think—
> Which I protest against—I am assisted
> By wicked powers.   (V.iii.85)

The "chapel" setting is necessary, for we attend the resurrection of a supposedly buried person; the solemnity is at least half funereal. Much is involved in the phrase "wicked powers": we watch no act of necromancy. The "magic" (V.iii.39), if magic it be, is a white magic; shall we say, a natural magic; the living opposite of the Ghost in

[2] A yet more relevant comparison with Yeats might adduce his drama *Resurrection*. Compare also the statue-interest of Ibsen's latest plays.

Hamlet hideously breaking his tomb's "ponderous and marble jaws" (I.iv.50). The difference is that between Prospero's powers in *The Tempest* and those of Marlowe's Doctor Faustus or the Weird Sisters in *Macbeth*. The distinction in Shakespeare's day was important and further driven home by Paulina's:

> It is requir'd
> You do awake your faith. Then, all stand still;
> Or those that think it is unlawful business
> I am about, let them depart.
>
> (V.iii.94)

The key word "faith" enlists New Testament associations, but to it Paulina adds a potency more purely Shakespearean: music. Shakespeare's use of music, throughout his main antagonist to tempestuous tragedy, reaches a newly urgent precision at Cerimon's restoration of Thaisa and Pericles' reunion with Marina. Here it functions as the specifically releasing agent:

> *Paulina.*   Music, awake her: strike! [*music sounds*]
> 'Tis time; descend; be stone no more; approach;
> Strike all that look upon with marvel. Come;
> I'll fill your grave up: stir, nay, come away;
> Bequeath to death your numbness, for from him
> Dear life redeems you. You perceive she stirs:
>
> [*Hermione comes down*]
>
> Start not; her actions shall be holy as
> You hear my spell is lawful; do not shun her
> Until you see her die again, for then
> You kill her double. Nay, present your hand:
> When she was young you woo'd her; now in age
> Is she become the suitor?
>
> *Leontes.*   O! she's warm.
> If this be magic, let it be an art
> Lawful as eating.
>
> (V.iii.98)

"Redeems" (cf. "ransomed" at V.ii.16), "holy" and "lawful" continue earlier emphases. The concreteness of "fill your grave up" has analogies in Shelley's *Witch of Atlas* (LXIX–LXXI) and the empty sepulcher of the New

Testament. Such resurrections are imaged as a reinfusing of the dead body with life. Hermione's restoration not only has nothing to do with black magic; it is not even transcendental. It exists in warm human actuality (cf. *Pericles*, V.i.154): hence our earlier emphases on warmth and breath; and now on "eating" too. It is, indeed, part after all of "great creating nature"; no more, and no less; merely another miracle from the great power, the master artist of creation, call it what you will, nature or eternity, Apollo or—as in the New Testament—"the living God". . . .

. . . *The Winter's Tale* may seem a rambling, perhaps an untidy, play; its anachronisms are vivid, its geography disturbing. And yet Shakespeare offers nothing greater in tragic psychology, humor, pastoral, romance, and that which tops them all and is, except for *Pericles*, new. The unity of thought is more exact than appears: it was Sicily, at first sight ill suited to the somber scenes here staged, that gave us the myth of Proserpine or Persephone. The more profound passages are perhaps rather evidence of what is beating behind or within the creative genius at work than wholly successful ways of printing purpose on an average audience's, or an average reader's, mind; but the passages are there, and so is the purpose, though to Shakespeare it need not have been defined outside his drama. That drama, however, by its very enigma, its unsolved and yet uncompromising statement, throws up —as in small compass did the little flower-dialogue too— a vague, numinous, sense of mighty powers, working through both the natural order and man's religious consciousness, that preserve, in spite of all appearance, the good. Orthodox tradition is used, but it does not direct; a pagan naturalism is used too. The Bible has been an influence; so have classical myth and Renaissance pastoral;[3] but the greatest influence was Life itself, that creating and protecting deity whose superhuman presence and powers the drama labors to define.

[3] And, it would seem, Greek drama too, especially Sophocles', wherein a tyrant is punished like Leontes by the sudden loss of his son (*Antigone*) and a child exposed like Perdita (*Oedipus*).

Wolfgang Clemen

From *The Development of Shakespeare's Imagery*

Of Shakespeare's romances *The Winter's Tale* shows the widest range of imagery. It embraces romantic and poetical imagery (as becoming to a "romance") as well as drastic and realistic imagery of the workaday world. The more intellectual types of imagery by which passion and thought express themselves are also represented, as well as the subtle and complex images that derive their effect from condensation and ambiguity. Mr. Bethell has made the acute observation (which he has illustrated by well-selected examples) that in *The Winter's Tale* we find a use of imagery and conceit more Jacobean than Elizabethan.[1] Thus Shakespeare's imagery does not only develop along the lines of Shakespeare's artistic evolution, but it also reflects the changes which we can trace in the transition of poetic style from the Elizabethan to the Jacobean period.

The Winter's Tale reveals in several respects an essentially Shakespearean tendency which we can trace throughout his whole dramatic career and which becomes more

From *The Development of Shakespeare's Imagery* by Wolfgang Clemen. Cambridge, Mass.: Harvard University Press; London: Methuen & Co., Ltd., 1951. Reprinted by permission of Harvard University Press and Methuen & Co., Ltd.

[1] S. L. Bethell, *The Winter's Tale, A Study*, London, Staples Press, 1947, p. 21.

and more conspicuous toward its end: the endeavor to establish a balance between opposites, never to give only one color without supplementing it by a complementary color, never to yield to one specific mood without contrasting it by other entirely different moods and spheres. This desire always to create a complex, round, and full picture partly accounts for Shakespeare's masterly faculty to blend various genres, sources, and elements into a new organic whole. It is not only brought out by his maturer technique of characterization but becomes evident in almost all aspects and features of his art. Imagery, in this connection, is a considerable help in securing this balance and complexity of which *The Winter's Tale* is a good example.

The imagery in the first three acts of the play which so much resemble a tragedy is set off distinctly from the imagery in the "romance" of the fourth act, where we again can trace various contrasting patterns. Compared to the fourth act, the images in that first part are shorter and more thinly spread all over the text. We have more single metaphors than in the fourth act, in which the images appear more in clusters, are more compact, stand out from the context more colorfully and strikingly and (in a longer passage) often crowd so closely that the effect and the impression of this passage seems to lie solely in the imagery. In the first part, on the other hand, the imagery, being more subsidiary, has rather the function of being an expression for thought and passion, whereas in the fourth part the imagery seems largely to have been introduced for its own sake.

It could also be said that in the first acts, the imagery is more "subterranean" and subordinate; every now and then, from this hidden stream, images rise up to the surface and tinge the language, sometimes only by way of metaphor. This subterranean flow of imagery not only finds its expression in a chain of iterative imagery, but also in the associative interrelation of images. Leontes' aside, for example, in I.ii.180, "I am angling now, . . ." gives rise, fourteen lines later, to "And his pond fish'd . . ." (I.ii.195), which may have also been suggested by "sluic'd" in the preceding line.

In the first act Leontes' growing obsession is pictured by Shakespeare through a series of disease-images and related imagery which express poisoning, disgust, and dirt. In the long passage spoken by Leontes after Polixenes and Hermione have left, Leontes confesses

> many thousand on's
> Have the disease, and feel't not (I.ii.206)

the disease of which he had before said "Physic for't there is none" (I.ii.200). This, at the same time, is self-revealing and possesses dramatic irony [2] as well as the other lines at the beginning of this speech:

> and I
> Play too, but so disgraced a part, whose issue
> Will hiss me to my grave: contempt and clamor
> Will be my knell.
>
> (I.ii.187)

Later, in the same scene, Camillo asks him to be "cured of this diseased opinion" (I.ii.296) and retorts to Leontes' false assumption of his "infected" wife "who does infect her?" (I.ii.306). The disease-imagery links up with the notion of taint and stinging things. Shortly after Camillo's question Leontes speaks the following words, which also contain dramatic irony:

> *Leontes.* Make that thy question, and go rot!
> Dost think I am so muddy, so unsettled,
> To appoint myself in this vexation, sully
> The purity and whiteness of my sheets,
> Which to preserve is sleep, which being
> Is goads, thorns, nettles, tails of wasps,
>
> (I.ii.325)

In the next scene this collocation of disease, of stinging and

---

[2] Another example of dramatic irony being expressed through an image occurs in II.iii.151:
"*Leon.* I am a feather for each wind that blows."

and poison [3] becomes more obvious. Note the following
lines spoken by Leontes:

> There may be in the cup
> A spider steep'd, and one may drink, depart,
> And yet partake no venom, for his knowledge
> Is not infected: but if one present
> The abhorr'd ingredient to his eye, make known
> How he hath drunk, he cracks his gorge, his sides,
> With violent hefts. I have drunk, and seen the
>   spider.

(II.i.39)

The dramatic and structural significance of this image
should be noted. For it is the first time Leontes builds up
a full image, all the more striking as Leontes' hasty diction
does not usually allow of the elaboration of images. The
directness and realism with which this image of the spider
in the cup is presented and the way Leontes turns it into
a personal experience, expressed by the laconic ending
"I have drunk, and seen the spider," bring home to us the
brutal and naked force of Leontes' self-deceiving obsession,
the sudden growth of which we witnessed in the preceding
scene. This is, moreover, the first longer speech we hear
of Leontes after he has reappeared in the second act.
Shakespeare could scarcely have found a more powerful
means of reminding us of what we saw in the first act and to
show that Leontes is now completely ruled by his jealousy,
which has grown beyond doubt.

That the disease-metaphor creeps into the language of
other characters,[4] too, is the usual Shakespearean process.

[3] It should be mentioned that previous to Leontes' above-quoted
words is Camillo's refusal to use "poison."

[4] From Camillo's renewed reference to "a sickness / which puts some
of us in distemper, but / I cannot name the disease" (I.ii.385) Polixenes
takes over the image and asks: "A sickness caught of me, and yet I
well!" (I.ii.399). The imprecation pronounced by him shortly after-
ward also derives from the disease-metaphor, "O, then my best blood
turn / To an infected jelly" (I.ii.418). When Paulina, in the second
scene of the second act, tries to get access to Leontes, she says: "I /
Do come with words as medicinal as true, / Honest as either, to purge

The disease-imagery is, of course, suspended in the fourth act, but in the fifth act there is an echo of it, though now in a contrary sense, in Leontes' wish:

> The blessed gods
> Purge all infection from our air whilst you
> Do climate here!
>
> (V.i.168)

As has already been said, the imagery in the first acts is generally in the way of metaphor. In many cases we have what may be called "sunken images." This thinned-out imagery corresponds in some way to Leontes' barren and restless style of arguing, to his becoming more and more isolated from the world.[5]

There is, however, in the first three acts, one other instance of a developed and extended image which deserves discussion. After the news of Hermione's supposed death Paulina exhorts Leontes to betake him

> To nothing but despair. A thousand knees
> Ten thousand years together, naked, fasting,
> Upon a barren mountain, and still winter
> In storm perpetual, could not move the gods
> To look that way thou wert.
>
> (IIIi.ii.208)

This magnificent and terrible image marks another decisive stage of the tragic development in the first three acts, it expresses the sense of Leontes' irretrievable guilt, and

---

him of that humor / That presses him from sleep" (II.iii.35–38). To which may be added her contrasting of Leontes' rotten opinion to the soundness of oak or stone (II.iii.88). The disease-imagery even spreads over to Hermione, who in III.ii.95–96 confesses: "from his presence / I am barr'd, like one infectious." Mr. Bethell refers to the disease-image on p. 80, *op. cit.*, whereas Professor Spurgeon does not seem to consider it as "a leading motive," mentioning it only incidentally (*Shakespeare's Imagery*, p. 306).

[5] Dr. Tillyard says: "Leontes' world is marvelously expressed by the hot and twisted language he uses" (*Shakespeare's Last Plays*, p. 76).

its effect upon us is the more forcible as it is the only fully executed image in this scene. At the same time, it forebodes the storm of the next scene.

The manner in which this storm is pictured in III.iii also deserves attention. For it is seen from two quite different angles. The Mariner's "the skies look grimly / And threaten present blusters. . . . The heavens . . . frown upon's." (III.iii.4), and Antigonus' similar references [6] imply the usual tempest-symbolism, whereas the Clown's prose observations on the storm express a far more realistic point of view:

> . . . now the ship boring the moon with her mainmast, and anon swallowed with yeast and froth, as you'd thrust a cork into a hogshead. . . . But to make an end of the ship, to see how the sea flapdragoned it: . . .
>
> (III.iii.91)

Dr. Tillyard has noted the abrupt transition from the melodramatic dream world of Antigonus to the old shepherd's world of "common humanity." [7] The imagery, to some extent, may illustrate this by the very different representation of the same thing.

To call the play a romance is fully justified only by the fourth and fifth acts. In the fourth act, nature bursts into life with extraordinary wealth and color. But for this strong country atmosphere in its pastoral setting we are prepared during the first acts by occasional touches. The second scene opens with

> Nine changes of the watery star have been
> The shepherd's note since we have left our throne.
>
> (I.ii.1)

And there is other nature imagery spread over the first

---

[6] "The storm begins: . . . The day frowns more and more. . . . I never saw / The heavens so dim by day. . . ." (III.iii.48, 53, 54).
[7] E. M. W. Tillyard, *Shakespeare's Last Plays*, p. 77.

scenes [8] which can be said to prepare and forebode the pastoral romance of the fourth act.[9]

As this fourth act (especially scenes iii and iv) has already been fully commented upon by various distinguished critics, a few remarks may suffice to recall Shakespeare's achievement here. It is, perhaps, the best example for Shakespeare's art of combining several moods and styles. Mr. Bethell has well demonstrated how that typical "juxtaposition of the timeless world of romance and the contemporary scene" is already conveyed to us in Autolycus' song which forms the beginning of scene iii.[10] It not only blends various styles (Elizabethan, Jacobean, and metaphysical); it also brings the "ideal world of romance" into relation with the very real world of everyday life and interconnects the contrasted spheres of natural beauty and of "the nasty sneak thief." It is interesting to note that a similar juxtaposition recurs in the next scene. Autolycus sings:

> Lawn as white as driven snow;
> Cypress black as e'er was crow;
> Gloves as sweet as damask roses;
> Masks for faces and for noses;
> Bugle bracelet, necklace amber,
> Perfume for a lady's chamber;
> Golden quoifs and stomachers,
> For my lads to give their dears;
> Pins and poking-sticks of steel,
> What maids lack from head to heel:
> Come buy of me, come;

(IV.iv.220)

The items from Autolycus' peddler's pack are here compared to things which suggest the imagery of Elizabethan lyrics: white as driven snow, sweet as damask roses. And

[8] For example, G. Wilson Knight, *The Crown of Life*, p. 88.

[9] In this connection, especially the beginning of the third act should be noted; Mr. Bethell considers this short scene as "a turning point in the play" (*op. cit.* p. 82). See also Dr. Tillyard, *loc. cit.* p. 76.

[10] Bethell, *op. cit.* p. 44, "The Meaning of a Song."

thus a romantic note is struck in this prosaic catalogue of
trifles and petty stuff. But all this cheap knickknackery,
sold and broken up by Autolycus and spread all over the
scene, gives much color and a homely and realistic flavor
to this peasants' idyl. Before Autolycus even enters, his
wares are announced by the servant: "he has ribbons of all
the colors i' the rainbow; points more than all the lawyers
in Bohemia can learnedly handle, though they come to
him by the gross: inkles, caddisses, cambrics, lawns. . . ."
(IV.iv.205). In a certain way, as early as in IV.iii, the
Clown's enumeration of all the items he is to buy for the
sheep-shearing introduces this varied and solid picture of
village-life atmosphere:

> Let me see; what am I to buy for our sheep-shearing
> feast? Three pound of sugar, five pound of currants,
> rice. . . . I must have saffron to color the warden pies;
> mace; dates?—none, that's out of my note; nutmegs,
> seven; a race or two of ginger, but that I may beg;
> four pound of prunes, and as many of raisins o' the
> sun.

> (IV.iii.37)

There are other small touches which help build up and
sustain this atmosphere in the next scene: the references
to milking time, to the kiln-hole, to the "grange or mill,"
and the Servant's announcement of the "three carters,
three shepherds, three neatherds, three swineherds" who
want to perform a dance "which the wenches say is a
gallimaufry of gambols." Autolycus by his absurd but
credulously believed ballads, adds to this picture a tinge of
quaintness and strangeness, e.g., when he speaks of the
usurer's wife who "longed to eat adders' heads and toads
carbonadoed" (IV.iv.265).

We become aware of the wide range of imagery in this
scene if we turn from the prose [11] of these adders' heads
and toads carbonadoed to the exquisite music of Perdita's

---

[11] Note how the change between prose and poetry in *The Winter's
Tale* also helps to emphasize the contrasting of spheres.

and Florizel's lines. For, indeed, imagery, diction, and the
music of the verse here combine and go together to build
up some of the most perfect pages Shakespeare has ever
written. The close amalgamation of verse and imagery
may best be seen in that beautiful passage where Florizel
compares Perdita to a wavelike movement of the language:

> when you do dance, I wish you
> A wave o' the sea, that you might ever do
> Nothing but; move still, still so,
> And own no other function.
>
> (IV.iv.140)

And has ever what we may call a conceit been uttered
in a language more natural, more spontaneous, and more
unaffected than in these lines occurring at the end of
Perdita's famous flower-speech:

> *Perdita.*   O, these I lack,
>   To make you garlands of; and my sweet friend
>   To strew him o'er and o'er.
>
> *Florizel.*   What, like a corse?
>
> *Perdita.* No, like a bank for love to lie and play on
>   Not like a corse; or if, not to be buried,
>   But quick and in mine arms. . . .
>
> (IV.iv.127)

We scarcely even notice that this is a conceit, for the
language flows on so naturally. But comparing this to any
conceit from the early plays we realize the development
Shakespeare has passed through until he reached this
stage.

Likewise, the economical, unobtrusive use of mythological names in Perdita's and Florizel's language may be
noted. These names of antique gods, to be sure, heighten
the tone of pastoral idyl, and remind us of the fact that
both Perdita and Florizel are of princely origin. But the
allusions to mythology appear here not as rhetorical orna-

ment,[12] for it seems the most natural thing that the lovers
should think of Flora, of the green Neptune, of "the
fire-robed god, / Golden Apollo" (IV.iv.29), and when
Perdita apostrophizes Proserpina we entirely forget the
rhetorical origin of this device,[13] so original is the way in
which it is tied up with the context:

> Now, my fair'st friend,
> I would I had some flowers o' the spring that might
> Become your time of day; and yours, and yours,
> That wear upon your virgin branches yet
> Your maidenheads growing: O Proserpina,
> For the flowers now, that frighted thou let's fall
> From Dis's waggon! daffodils,
> That comes before the swallow dares, and take
> The winds of March with beauty . . .
>
> (IV.iv.112)

Another example of how traditional patterns of expression
falling under the heading "imagery" appear now in a
much refined manner is Florizel's declaration:

> I take thy hand, this hand,
> As soft as dove's down and as white as it,
> Or Ethiopian's tooth, or the fann'd snow that's bolted
> By the northern blasts twice o'er.
>
> (IV.iv.366)

It had been habitual for the Elizabethan lovers in Shakespeare's early plays to compare their beloved's eyes, skin,
hair, or hands, to various beautiful things, and the device
of piling up, on such occasions, several comparisons, is an
old one. "As soft as dove's down and as white as it" is
quite in this style. But the next two lines surprise us by the
strangeness and novelty of the images, the simile becom-

---

[12] Cf. the abundant and not always fitting use of mythological names
in *Cymbeline*.

[13] Cf. the apostrophes in *Cymbeline* which are mostly in rhetorical
manner.

ing, moreover, as Mr. Bethell has pointed out, more complex by the introduction of the metaphor of "bolting." [14] All this is no longer typical Elizabethan style, but an anticipation of Donne.

It may be objected that by merely noting down all these small details and tiny touches we do not get much further in understanding the real meaning of the play, in penetrating to the core of the matter. There certainly is some truth in this warning. For we are apt to get too much absorbed by the examination of the minutiae and may lose hold of the full and rounded view of a Shakespearean drama. But a study of this kind can never be more than one of several approaches which we must in the end coordinate in order to arrive at a more comprehensive appreciation of the play. And then we discover that there is more in the details of imagery than we at first sight anticipated. This holds good of *The Winter's Tale*, too. The contrasting and blending of the ideal romance world with the realistically and drastically represented village life [15] is more than a mere collocation of different atmospheres, and contains a deeper meaning which in fact leads us a little nearer to the play's central problem. Shakespeare evidently wanted to show that the renewal and regeneration of a decaying world as symbolized by the Perdita-Florizel episode in the fourth act must have roots in the firm reality and simplicity of the country life as well as in the more refined court world.[16] "Country and court are necessary to each other, Shakespeare seems to imply, the sober virtues of the one and the graces of the other compounding a perfect whole," as Mr. Bethell has put it. And this necessary union is again indicated by the imagery which at the same time possesses dramatic

---

[14] Bethell, *op. cit.*, p. 23. "Bolted" introduces a metaphor into the simile and supplies the further image of "wheaten flour the snow is made purer by being twice sifted as wheaten flour is sifted of its impurities."

[15] A German critic has well compared the fourth act to a combination of Romanticism with a Dutch painting by Teniers, representing a peasants' fair (Gustav Landauer, *Shakespeare*, 1923, p. 257).

[16] For this cf. Chapters 3 and 4 of the second part of Mr. Bethell's study. For the idea of rebirth see also Tillyard, *op. cit.*, p. 42.

irony,[17] for the speaker Polixenes, by his subsequent action against his son, himself deviates from the procedure which he recommends here as an organic law:

> You see, sweet maid, we marry
> A gentler scion to the wildest stock,
> And make conceive a bark of baser kind
> By bud of nobler race: this is an art
> Which does mend nature, change it rather, but
> The art itself is nature.

(IV.iv.92)

We have above noted the gay display of all the trifling, trivial knickknacks, so much coveted by the peasants. This, again, does more than merely to create atmosphere if we look at the import of the whole scene. For it is to form a significant contrast to the love-making between Florizel and Perdita which goes on in the midst of this merry bustle and is on such an entirely different plane. It is Florizel himself who avows

> Old sir, I know
> She prizes not such trifles as these are:
> The gifts she looks from me are pack'd and lock'd
> Up in my heart; which I have given already,
> But not deliver'd.

(IV.iv.360)

Thus Shakespeare subsequently utilizes Autolycus' trifles in order to suggest his favorite theme of appearance and reality that, in some way, also runs through *The Winter's Tale*.

[17] See Bethell, *op. cit.*, p. 27.

Suggested References

The number of possible references is vast and grows alarmingly. (The *Shakespeare Quarterly* devotes a substantial part of one issue each year to a list of the previous year's work, and *Shakespeare Survey*—an annual publication—includes a substantial review of recent scholarship, as well as an occasional essay surveying a few decades of scholarship on a chosen topic.) Russell Fraser, the editor of the Signet Classic *King Lear,* offers this warning: "These comments may be ventured, regarding the titles listed here, and the critical selections above. First, no work of criticism, however excellent in itself, is to be taken as rivaling in importance, much less as supplanting, the thing it criticizes. The play's the thing! and not the commentaries thereon. Second, any work of criticism, and particularly to the degree that it is excellent, ought to be scrutinized with a cold eye whenever it pretends to the making of a definitive judgment. In the interpretation of Shakespeare, no comment is sacrosanct or final. Let the reader beware, therefore; and let him also take heart. 'Judgment, like other faculties, is improved by practice, and its advancement hindered by submission to dictatorial decisions, as the memory grows torpid by the use of a table book.' Thus Dr. Johnson."

1. Shakespeare's Times

Byrne, M. St. Clare. *Elizabethan Life in Town and Country.* Rev. ed. New York: Barnes & Noble, Inc., 1961. Chapters on manners, beliefs, education, etc., with illustrations.

Craig, Hardin. *The Enchanted Glass: the Elizabethan Mind in Literature.* New York and London: Oxford University Press, 1936. The Elizabethan intellectual climate.

Nicoll, Allardyce (ed.). *The Elizabethans.* London: Cambridge University Press, 1957. An anthology of Elizabethan writings, especially valuable for its illustrations from paintings, title pages, etc.

Shakespeare's England. Oxford: Clarendon Press, 1916. 2 vols. A large collection of scholarly essays on a wide variety of topics (e.g., astrology, costume, gardening, horsemanship), with special attention to Shakespeare's references to these topics.

Tillyard, E. M. W. *The Elizabethan World Picture.* London: Chatto & Windus, 1943; New York: The Macmillan Company, 1944. A brief account of some Elizabethan ideas of the universe.

Wilson, John Dover (ed.). *Life in Shakespeare's England.* 2nd ed. New York: The Macmillan Company, 1913. An anthology of Elizabethan writings on the countryside, superstition, education, the court, etc.

2. SHAKESPEARE

Bentley, Gerald E. *Shakespeare: A Biographical Handbook.* New Haven, Conn.: Yale University Press, 1961. The facts about Shakespeare, with virtually no conjecture intermingled.

Bradby, Anne (ed.). *Shakespeare Criticism, 1919–1935.* London: Oxford University Press, 1936. A small anthology of excellent essays on the plays.

Bush, Geoffrey Douglas. *Shakespeare and the Natural Condition.* Cambridge, Mass.: Harvard University Press, 1956; London: Oxford University Press, 1956. A short, sensitive account of Shakespeare's view of "Nature," touching most of the works.

Chute, Marchette. *Shakespeare of London.* E. P. Dutton & Co., Inc., 1949. A readable biography fused with portraits of Stratford and London life.

Clemen, Wolfgang H. *The Development of Shakespeare's Imagery*. Cambridge, Mass.: Harvard University Press, 1951. (Originally published in German, 1936.) A temperate account of a subject often abused.

Chambers, E. K. *William Shakespeare: A Study of Facts and Problems*. London: Oxford University Press, 1930. 2 vols. An invaluable, detailed reference work; not for the casual reader.

Craig, Hardin. *An Interpretation of Shakespeare*. New York: Citadel Press, 1948. A scholar's book designed for the layman. Comments on all the works.

Dean, Leonard F. (ed.). *Shakespeare: Modern Essays in Criticism*. New York: Oxford University Press, 1957. Mostly mid-twentieth-century critical studies, covering Shakespeare's artistry.

Granville-Barker, Harley. *Prefaces to Shakespeare*. Princeton, N.J.: Princeton University Press, 1946–47. 2 vols. Essays on ten plays by a scholarly man of the theater.

Harbage, Alfred. *As They Liked It*. New York: The Macmillan Company, 1947. A sensitive, long essay on Shakespeare, morality, and the audience's expectations.

Smith, D. Nichol (ed.). *Shakespeare Criticism*. New York: Oxford University Press, 1916. A selection of criticism from 1623 to 1840, ranging from Ben Jonson to Thomas Carlyle.

Spencer, Theodore. *Shakespeare and the Nature of Man*. New York: The Macmillan Company, 1942. Shakespeare's plays in relation to Elizabethan thought.

Stoll, Elmer Edgar. *Shakespeare and Other Masters*. Cambridge, Mass.: Harvard University Press, 1940; London: Oxford University Press, 1940. Essays on tragedy, comedy, and aspects of dramaturgy, with special reference to some of Shakespeare's plays.

Traversi, D. A. *An Approach to Shakespeare*. Rev. ed. New York: Doubleday & Co., Inc., 1956. An analysis of the plays, beginning with words, images, and themes, rather than with characters.

Van Doren, Mark. *Shakespeare*. New York: Henry Holt & Company, Inc., 1939. Brief, perceptive readings of all of the plays.

Whitaker, Virgil K. *Shakespeare's Use of Learning*. San Marino, Calif.: Huntington Library, 1953. A study of the relation of Shakespeare's reading to his development as a dramatist.

3. SHAKESPEARE'S THEATER

Adams, John Cranford. *The Globe Playhouse*. Rev. ed. New York: Barnes & Noble, Inc., 1961. A detailed conjecture about the physical characteristics of the theater Shakespeare often wrote for.

Beckerman, Bernard. *Shakespeare at the Globe, 1599–1609*. New York: The Macmillan Company, 1962. On the playhouse and on Elizabethan dramaturgy, acting, and staging.

Chambers, E. K. *The Elizabethan Stage*. New York: Oxford University Press, 1923. 4 vols. Reprinted with corrections, 1945. An indispensable reference work on theaters, theatrical companies, and staging at court.

Harbage, Alfred. *Shakespeare's Audience*. New York: Columbia University Press, 1941; London: Oxford University Press, 1941. A study of the size and nature of the theatrical public.

Hodges, C. Walter. *The Globe Restored*. London: Ernest Benn, Ltd., 1953; New York: Coward-McCann, Inc., 1954. A well-illustrated and readable attempt to reconstruct the Globe Theatre.

Nagler, A. M. *Shakespeare's Stage*. Tr. by Ralph Manheim. New Haven, Conn.: Yale University Press, 1958. An excellent brief introduction to the physical aspect of the playhouse.

Smith, Irwin. *Shakespeare's Globe Playhouse*. New York: Charles Scribner's Sons, 1957. Chiefly indebted to J. C. Adams' controversial book, with additional material and scale drawings for model-builders.

Venezky, Alice S. *Pageantry on the Shakespearean Stage*. New York: Twayne Publishers, Inc., 1951. An examination of spectacle in Elizabethan drama.

4. MISCELLANEOUS REFERENCE WORKS

Abbott, E. A. *A Shakespearean Grammar*. New edition. New York: The Macmillan Company, 1877. An examination of differences between Elizabethan and modern grammar.

Bartlett, John. *A New and Complete Concordance . . . to . . . Shakespeare*. New York: The Macmillan Company, 1894. An index to most of Shakespeare's words.

Bullough, Geoffrey. *Narrative and Dramatic Sources of Shakespeare*. New York: Columbia University Press, 1957–; London: Routledge & Kegan Paul, Ltd., 1957–. 4 vols. Vols. 5 and 6 in preparation. A collection of many of the books Shakespeare drew upon.

Greg, W. W. *The Shakespeare First Folio*. New York and London: Oxford University Press, 1955. A detailed yet readable history of the first collection (1623) of Shakespeare's plays.

Kökeritz, Helge. *Shakespeare's Names*. New Haven, Conn.: Yale University Press, 1959; London: Oxford University Press, 1960. A guide to the pronunciation of some 1,800 names appearing in Shakespeare.

————. *Shakespeare's Pronunciation*. New Haven, Conn.: Yale University Press, 1953; London: Oxford University Press, 1953. Contains much information about puns and rhymes.

Linthicum, Marie C. *Costume in the Drama of Shakespeare and His Contemporaries*. New York and London: Oxford University Press, 1936. On the fabrics and dress of the age, and references to them in the plays.

Muir, Kenneth. *Shakespeare's Sources*. London: Methuen & Co., Ltd., 1957. Vol. 2 in preparation. The first volume, on the comedies and tragedies, attempts to ascertain what books were Shakespeare's sources, and what use he made of them.

Onions, C. T. *A Shakespeare Glossary*. London: Oxford University Press, 1911; 2nd ed., rev., with enlarged addenda, 1953. Definitions of words (or senses of words) now obsolete.

Partridge, Eric. *Shakespeare's Bawdy*. Rev. ed. New York: E. P. Dutton & Co., Inc., 1955; London: Routledge & Kegan Paul, Ltd., 1955. A glossary of bawdy words and phrases.

Shakespeare Quarterly. See headnote to Suggested References.

Shakespeare Survey. See headnote to Suggested References.

5. THE WINTER'S TALE

Bentley, Gerald E. "Shakespeare and the Blackfriars Theatre," *Shakespeare Survey,* I (1948), 38–50.

Bethell, S. L. *The Winter's Tale: A Study*. London: Staples Press, Ltd., 1947.

Bryant, J. A., Jr. "Shakespeare's Allegory: *The Winter's Tale,*" *Sewanee Review,* LXIII (1955), 202–22.

Coghill, Nevill. "Six Points of Stage-Craft in *The Winter's Tale,*" *Shakespeare Survey,* XI (1958), 31–41.

Edwards, Philip. "Shakespeare's Romances: 1900–1957," *Shakespeare Survey,* XI (1958), 1–18.

Frye, Northrop. *Anatomy of Criticism*. Princeton, N.J.: Princeton University Press; London: Oxford University Press, 1957.

———. "The Argument of Comedy," *English Institute Essays, 1948*. New York: Columbia University Press, 1949.

———. "Recognition in *The Winter's Tale,*" *Essays on Shakespeare and Elizabethan Drama,* ed. Richard Hosley. Columbia, Missouri: University of Missouri Press, 1962.

Greenlaw, E. "Shakepeare's Pastorals," *Studies in Philology*, XIII (1916), 122–54.

Hoeniger, F. D. "The Meaning of *The Winter's Tale*," *University of Toronto Quarterly*, XX (1950), 11–26.

James, D. G. *Scepticism and Poetry*. New York: Barnes & Noble, Inc., 1960; London: George Allen & Unwin, Ltd., 1937.

Knight, G. Wilson. *The Crown of Life*. New York and London: Oxford University Press, 1947. Part of this material is reprinted above.

————. *The Shakespearian Tempest*. New York and London: Oxford University Press, 1932.

Lawlor, John. "*Pandosto* and the Nature of Dramatic Romance," *Philological Quarterly*, XLI (1962), 96–113.

Leavis, F. R. "A Criticism of Shakespeare's Last Plays," *Scrutiny*, X (1942), 339–45. Reprinted in *The Common Pursuit*, London: Chatto & Windus, Ltd., 1952; Penguin Books, Ltd., 1962.

Pettet, E. C. *Shakespeare and the Romance Tradition*. London: Staples Press, Ltd., 1950.

Spencer, Theodore. "Appearance and Reality in Shakespeare's Last Plays," *Modern Philology*, XXXIX (1942), 265–74.

Strachey, Lytton. "Shakespeare's Final Period," in *Books and Characters*. London: Chatto & Windus, Ltd.; New York: Harcourt, Brace & Co., Inc., 1922. Reprinted in *Literary Essays*. London: Chatto & Windus, Ltd., 1948; New York, Harcourt, Brace & Co., Inc., 1949.

Tillyard, E. M. W. *Shakespeare's Last Plays*. London: Chatto & Windus, 1938. Part of this material is reprinted above.

Tinkler, F. C. "The Winter's Tale," *Scrutiny*, V (1937), 344–64.

Traversi, D. A. *Shakespeare: The Last Phase*. New York: Harcourt, Brace & Co., Inc., 1955; London: Hollis & Carter, 1954.

THE SIGNET CLASSIC SHAKESPEARE

The works of Shakespeare in superlatively edited paperbound volumes. Under the general editorship of Sylvan Barnet, Chairman of the English Department of Tufts University, each volume features General Introduction by Dr. Barnet, special Introduction and Notes by an eminent Shakespearean scholar, critical commentary from past and contemporary authorities, and when possible, Shakespeare's original source material.

☐ **THE SONNETS.** Introduction by W. H. Auden
(#CD257—50¢)

☐ **ANTONY AND CLEOPATRA.** Edited by Barbara Everett
(#CT392—75¢)

☐ **AS YOU LIKE IT.** Edited by Albert Gilman
(#CT520—75¢)

☐ **HAMLET.** Edited by Edward Hubler   (#CT528—75¢)
☐ **JULIUS CAESAR.** Edited by William and Barbara Rosen
(#CT529—75¢)

☐ **KING LEAR.** Edited by Russell Fraser (#CD160—50¢)
☐ **MACBETH.** Edited by Sylvan Barnet (#CD161—50¢)
☐ **MEASURE FOR MEASURE.** Edited by S. Nagarajan
(#CT541—75¢)

☐ **A MIDSUMMER NIGHT'S DREAM.** Edited by Wolfgang
Clemen (#CT518—75¢)

☐ **MUCH ADO ABOUT NOTHING.** Edited by David Stevenson
(#CD173—50¢)

☐ **OTHELLO.** Edited by Alvin Kernan (#CD162—50¢)
☐ **RICHARD II.** Edited by Kenneth Muir (#CD163—50¢)
☐ **RICHARD III.** Edited by Mark Eccles (#CD175—50¢)
☐ **THE TEMPEST.** Edited by Robert Langbaum
(#CT527—75¢)

☐ **TITUS ANDRONICUS.** Edited by Sylvan Barnet
(#CD197—50¢)

☐ **TROILUS AND CRESSIDA.** Edited by Daniel Seltzer
(#CT477—75¢)

☐ **TWO GENTLEMEN OF VERONA.** Edited by Bertrand
Evans (#CD219—50¢)

☐ **THE WINTER'S TALE.** Edited by Frank Kermode
(#CD164—50¢)